CHANGE AND CONTINUITY
IN BRITISH SOCIETY

1800–1850

Richard Brown

Head of History

Houghton Regis Upper School

Bedfordshire

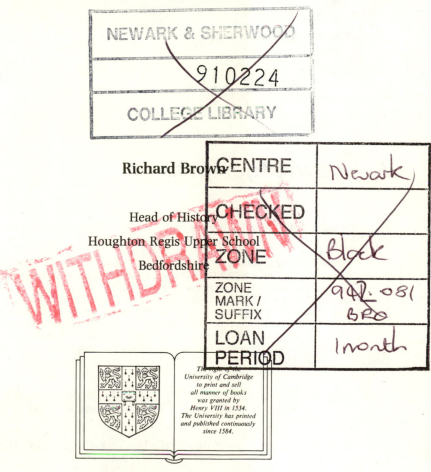

The right of the
University of Cambridge
to print and sell
all manner of books
was granted by
Henry VIII in 1534.
The University has printed
and published continuously
since 1584.

CAMBRIDGE UNIVERSITY PRESS

Cambridge   New York
New Rochelle   Melbourne   Sydney

Published by the Press Syndicate of the University of Cambridge
The Pitt Building, Trumpington Street, Cambridge CB2 1RP
32 East 57th Street, New York, NY 10022, USA
10 Stamford Road, Oakleigh, Melbourne 3166, Australia

First published 1987

Printed in Great Britain at the University Press, Cambridge

British Library cataloguing in publication data

Brown, Richard
  Change and continuity in British society
  1800–1850
  1. Great Britain – Social conditions
  – 19th century
  I. Title
  941.081   HN385

ISBN 0 521 31727 4

Acknowledgements

The author and publisher would like to thank the following for permission to reproduce extracts and illustrations:

1.2 G. E. *Mingay, Rural life in Victorian Britain*, William Heinemann Ltd; 1.3(c) Crown Copyright; p.59 Theatre Royal, Bury St Edmunds; 2.2 Croome Helm Limited; 2.7(a) Alexis de Tocqueville, *The Old Regime and the French Revolution*, Fontana Paperbacks, translated by S. Gilbert; 2.7(b) American Sociological Association, 1722 N Street, NW, Washington, DC 20036; 4.2 Mansell Collection; 5.2 E. M. Tucker, *Britain 1760–1914*, Edward Arnold (Publishers) Ltd; 5.5 G. Himmelfarb; 5.6 WEA Eastern District; 5.10 From 'Tocqueville: memoir on pauperism' pp.10–25 in *Tocqueville and Beaumont on Social Reform*, ed. and translated with and introduction by Seymour Drescher. Copyright © 1968 by Seymour Drescher. Reprinted by permission of Harper & Row, Publishers, Inc.; 5.11 Merlin Press; 7.13 Peter Coombs; 7.20 BBC Hulton Picture Library.

I wish to acknowledge the invaluable assistance given to me by CUP, and particularly Sally Taylor (Editor) and Stephanie Boyd, who piloted this, her first book, through the quicksands and shoals of schoolbook publishing.

Cover illustration: detail from 'Going to the Epsom Race by train', 'Third Class', from *Illustrated London News*, 1847.

Contents

for George Roper Mackender
1901–1984
whose roots in the Fens went
back long before the events
in this book

Introduction:
change and continuity 1800–1850

Preface

The changes that took place between 1800 and 1850 marked a fundamental shift in the development of Britain [**3.1(a) and (b)**]. Within a person's lifetime Britain was completely transformed. J. F. C. Harrison recently commented that,

> Possibly the only time parallel to the events of 1760–1830 is to be found in the Neolithic Age when man discovered how to become a settled agriculturalist and herdsman instead of a hunter and nomad.[1]

In 1800 Britain was a predominantly agrarian country, albeit one undergoing industrialisation, with farming as the main occupation. By 1850 it was the 'workshop of the world' with the Bradford woolmark and the Birmingham stamp as universal as 'made in Hong Kong' is today. Towns and cities replaced villages and hamlets as focal points of population. But this was more than just technological and economic change with the possibility of material abundance. Society became able to change its environment instead of being at nature's mercy. This led to changes in how people regarded themselves, their society and its organisation, the way they were ruled and their world-view. The old assumptions were questioned, challenged and radically changed. But this challenge was not unopposed. The forces of continuity retained their strength.

A   The historian, the sources and the concepts

I   The problem of objectivity and the charge of bias

> What needs to be said is not that one way of life is better than the other, but that this is a place of the most far-reaching conflict; that the historical record is not a simple one of neutral and inevitable technological change, but is also one of exploitation and of resistance to exploitation; and that values stood to be lost as well as gained.
> [E. P. Thompson][2]

So how do we look at the past? Narrative is central to historians. They can speak and write of earlier ages through the accounts and possessions of contemporaries. It is to the evidence that the historian must always return. But events and people have always aroused passions. Handloom weavers had pronounced views on the changes that were destroying their livelihood. It is in the *selection* of evidence that the problem of objectivity arises. If historians are looking for evidence to show the debilitating effects of change then it can be found – just as historians can find evidence for the beneficial nature of enclosure or factories or town growth. It is how historians use that evidence which is crucial.

You could easily think that there are only two views on the impact of economic change in Britain during the Industrial Revolution. The 'pessimists', beginning with Toynbee in the 1880s, through the Hammonds to E. J. Hobsbawm and E. P. Thompson today, emphasise the notion of social injustice and exploitation. The 'optimists', Sir John Clapham, Ashton and Hartwell among others, look at the beneficial effects of economic change.[3] There is always a danger that what is a continuing debate on the impact of change and continuity will become, in the popular imagination, a dialogue between good and evil.

How can historians come to almost diametrically opposed conclusions on the basis of the same or similar evidence? E. H. Carr stated that,

> The facts of history never come to us 'pure', since they do not and cannot exist in a pure form: they are always refracted through the mind of the recorder. It follows that when we take up a work of history, our first concern should be not with the facts which it contains but with the historian who wrote it.[4]

The questions which, when answered, resolve these problems are the most obvious of all – 'what is your authority for saying this?' and 'how do you know that this happened in the way that you say it happened?'. Historians are ultimately as accountable to the evidence and the correct way of reasoning from it as the practitioners of any body of knowledge. Objectivity in history is above all the balanced and fair assessment of the evidence.

2   A plethora of sources

In the words of Geoffrey Elton,

> Historical study is not the study of the past but the study of present traces of the past; if men have said, thought, done or suffered anything of which nothing exists, those things are as though they had

never been. The crucial element is the present evidence, not the fact of past existence[5]

It is, in any event, impossible in principle to report the full, detailed truth. It is simply not available. J. H. Hexter states that,

> Very few persons alive today will leave behind them when they die, any direct record whatever of any sound they uttered or any bodily movement they made, save, perhaps, as a voice and a speck in a roaring crowd . . . no man or woman in the entire past up to the 1880s left any audible record whatever of any sound they ever made[6]

It is upon visual, and particularly the proliferation of written, evidence that historians of the early to mid nineteenth century must rely. Much of this material was generated by central government. There were the Census returns [1.13(c)], the reports of Select Committees of both Houses of Parliament and the specially appointed Royal Commissions like those set up to look into the Poor Laws and Municipal Corporations. Parliamentary papers, especially the 'Blue Books', are of particular value in discussing social and economic conditions. From 1803, verbatim reports of parliamentary debates are available [6.17(a)–(c)]. Important though this material is, historians do not accept it uncritically. The membership of Select Committees and the witnesses examined could easily be unrepresentative, having a strong bias towards pre-selected evidence and forming inevitable conclusions. This is exemplified in the committee which examined the state of woollen manufacture in 1806 [4.3, 4.5, 4.6]. Royal Commissions, made up of 'experts', could be less partisan and examined their subjects less hurriedly. But even here preconceived views played an important role. Evidence collected could be contradictory and this could lead, as in the case of the Poor Law Royal Commission, to accepting only that evidence which supported its prejudices [see Chapter 5].

Much material on local county administration and jurisdiction together with family and estate records can be found in local record offices.[7] Local newspapers, some periodicals, gazetteers [1.13(b)] and directories [3.7(a) and (b)] can also be used and provide graphic illustration of local problems. Papers and periodicals do, however, have certain limitations. Provincial newspapers often took their news verbatim from *The Times*. Many of the local issues reported only take on real significance when viewed in the regional or national context. In many of these newspapers and periodicals it was middle class values that dominated, with working people only emerging as victims of disasters or as levelling agitators.

The middle class perspective is evident across a whole range of sources, particularly so in the 'social novel'. In Disraeli's *Sybil* or Charles Kingsley's *Alton Locke* the fictional details of the lives of working people reflect an observed rather than experienced assessment of the problems and behaviour of the working population. The same difficulty is found in the records of actual life. Historians rely on the Poor Law official, the magistrate, the philanthropist and journalist for much of their information. Workers – apart from the few exceptions who were sufficiently articulate to write autobiographies – emerged only when they threatened public order or when 'respectable' society had its conscience pricked by the revelation of conditions. This slant must always be kept in view when sifting through evidence. Eric Richards highlights the general problem:

> Landlords, factors, sheep-farmers, tacksmen, ministers, famine relief officials and radical spokesmen have almost totally dominated the story of the Highland Clearances to the exclusion of the people who constituted 95 per cent of the population of the region . . . the common people of the Highlands, like those elsewhere, have been careless of posterity: poor and mostly illiterate they have left little direct record of their lives[8]

But sources are *not* all written. W. G. Hoskins made the case for considering the changing physical environment:

> I am concerned with the ways in which men have cleared the natural woodlands; reclaimed marshland, fen and moor; created fields out of the wilderness; made lanes, roads and footpaths; laid out towns, built villages, hamlets, farmhouses and cottages; created country houses and their parks; dug mines and made canals and railways; in short, with everything that has altered the natural landscape.[9]

What are now familiar – factories, canals, railways, vast sprawling urban areas – were largely unknown in 1750. These changes are well documented in the maps and plans of the period [3.7(c)], in old prints [4.2], in early photographs and in the physical remains (such as buildings and machines). Hoskins will admit that initially,

> We have to go to the documents that are the historian's raw material and find out what happened to produce these results and when, and precisely how they came about.[10]

3 Change and continuity

John Miller begins his reflection on the concept of change with this statement:

> Ordinarily change is measured with reference to the permanent and is explained in terms of the permanent.[11]

In other words, historians explain changes by reference to the permanent, things that continue, things that have, in the context of a specific event, remained unaltered. It is how people reacted to or were affected by change that historians have tended to concentrate on. The reason for this emphasis lies, to some extent, in the human need to assess or measure the nature and value of change. Was a particular change beneficial or not? How can we judge particular changes?

There is also a difference between the historical understanding of the past and the contemporary experience of it. Change may well have impressed itself upon both contemporaries and later historians. But the notion of continuity was implicit in the 'moral economy', the naive agrarianism of the Chartist Land Plan and the snipings of William Cobbett. James Graham, a member of that 1806 Select Committee was not expressing a minority view when he said that,

> If the factory system were to exclude from the country the domestic system it would be dreadful indeed, for it is very pleasing in Yorkshire to see domestic clothiers living in a field, with their homesteads, rather than shut up in a street.

Historians are beginning to re-examine the chronology of change in this period and Malcolm Thomis is surely right when he says that,

> It is common to exaggerate both the speed of social change and the individual's sense of perspective on the events through which he is living and forget that a man is always living in what is for him the present day.[12]

Factories did not take over from outwork overnight – and anyway outwork was not as universal as some contemporaries believed. Towns did not spring up like mushrooms. People were aware that things were changing and their responses to those changes varied. It led to ambiguities, with Cobbett on the one hand deploring the economic changes, and yet on the other deciding that the hope for a better future lay with the industrial working classes and not the farmers. Change led to frustration, despair, anger, a fond longing for some mythical yet recent past [4.1]. But it also led to growth, increasing productivity, and growing power. Thomis continues,

> It is very clear that the majority who lived through the Industrial Revolution did not spend their time bemoaning the process of change which they were experiencing.

B   The environments of change

I   Revolutions in the economy

Britain's economic pre-eminence was stamped upon the contemporary imagination during the Great Exhibition of 1851. It symbolised British manufacturing and technological might. But however impressive Britain's industrial achievements were, they have to be seen in the context of the other economic revolutions.[13]

The population of England and Wales rose from about six million in 1700 to nearly nine million in 1801 and eighteen million by 1851. This was paralleled by a doubling of Scotland's population between 1801 and 1851 and Ireland's population reaching 8.2 million in 1841, before the catastrophic effects of the potato famines of that decade. From the 1780s the British Isles experienced an average annual population increase of between one and two per cent. The reasons for this growth are easily stated – a falling death rate and a steady or slightly rising birth rate. However, this fails to take into account local variations, especially the results of the appalling living conditions in the newer industrial centres. There were important regional differences as well. Population growth was uneven. In general terms areas with large-scale manufacturing industries grew faster than those concentrating on food production [3.3(a)].

Migration played an important part in this increase, especially after 1780. The Irish proved even more mobile than the English since there was little Irish industry to absorb the surplus population. There was a continuous stream of Irish unskilled labour into the industrial centres on the west coast of Britain. Much of this was seasonal with labourers planting their potatoes in the spring, leaving their families to look after the plot while they went to work in England on the railways or building the new towns, returning in the autumn to harvest their crop. Increasingly this flow became one of permanent settlement especially from the 1830s and after the famines of the mid 1840s. The Clearances in Highland Scotland of the 1780–1850 period also resulted in mass exodus to the industrial centres of Lowland Scotland, the industrial North and London.

In 1851 Henry Mayhew discovered men dressed in the rags of highland dress playing the bagpipes for the toss of a coin on the streets of London. People dispossessed in any part of the United Kingdom often ended up among the poorest social groups of urban life. Leaving Britain altogether was an increasingly attractive solution. Between 1820 and 1850 some 2.4 million chose to emigrate.

Dramatic though this growth was it was the impact of demographic growth that was truly revolutionary. Increasing population created increased demand for food and manufactured goods which could be produced by the reservoir of available labour. Once the cycle of increased population stimulating industrial and agrarian expansion had begun then the productive capacity of an evolving economy was liberated in a revolutionary way. Wages in towns increased. This acted as a magnet for the surrounding area with a consequent movement of the focal point of population from rural to urban settings. Expanding industries encouraged a higher birth rate; this occurred in both Yorkshire and Lancashire.[14]

Thomas Malthus, an influential demographic theorist, was one of a number of people who were suspicious of this increase in population. Malthus believed that the population would soon outstrip available resources and that increased famine and disease would bring the population under check. The demographic crisis in Ireland in the mid 1840s demonstrated the dangers of unfettered growth. That this did not occur as dramatically elsewhere owed much to the revolution in agricultural productivity.[15]

Between 1700 and 1830 a series of developments, many of which had their origins in the seventeenth century, resulted in a more rational use of much arable land. New crops like turnips and leguminous crops ended the need for land to be left fallow. Advances in iron production led to major advances in ploughing equipment, though it was not until after 1830 that labour-saving devices were widely used. Selective breeding increased both meat and dairy products. But it was the continued enclosure of vast areas of lighter land and the Clearances in Scotland that allowed the rationalisation of land usage. In fact the needs of the population pushed back the margins of arable land as never before – on to dubious land in the Mendips, on chalk escarpments and on the boulder clays of the Midland Plain. By 1820, twenty-five million quarters of corn were produced annually compared with fifteen million quarters sixty years before.

But this was barely enough. Britain ceased to be a major grain exporter. Bad harvests could push prices spiralling upwards – splendid for the farmer but distressing for the poor [see Chapter 2]. Good harvests and imports brought problems for farmers with their high mortgages, hence their successful demand for protection in 1815. Many farmers complained of 'depression' after 1815 through to the late 1830s. High costs certainly made wheat farming difficult when prices were low. But pastoral farmers were less vulnerable. Agriculture was capable of feeding Britain's growing population. Urban growth could not have occurred as quickly without assured food supplies. Good profits for many farmers meant money to spend on manufactured goods as well as for capital investment in industry. Without guaranteed food supplies changes could not have taken place elsewhere.

The revolution in industrial productivity also lasted for much of the eighteenth and early nineteenth centuries.[16] Important though developments in the textile industries were, especially the cotton industry, they were but one facet of economic change. Cast iron production had been revolutionised by 1750 with the widespread adoption of the 'coking' process and this growth continued with the application of the 'puddling and rolling' process after 1785. Iron rails, iron pots and iron tools became widespread. Coal production expanded after 1750 as the problems of drainage, ventilation and haulage were gradually solved. Bottlenecks in textile production led to technological advances in spinning and then weaving. But the importance of these developments lay in their mechanised production in the new environment of the mill and their concentration in Yorkshire and Lancashire. Iron, coal and textiles stimulated growth in other branches of manufacturing industry.

Parallel to changes in population, farming and industry were revolutions in inland communication – canals, and to a lesser extent roads after 1760, and railways after 1830 – the growth of financial institutions, growing trade and a changing economic philosophy with an emphasis on 'market forces'. These and other developments contributed to the overall nature of change by acting and reacting with each other. But none were planned or, at least initially, regulated by government. Historians often create a regularity, an order, or even an inevitability to changes that were unpredictable or, as one historian has written, 'bizarre'.

2   The changing landscape

Between 1750 and 1850 the physical appearance of Britain changed.[17] The pattern of field, stone-wall and hedgerow had already been established in northern and western England as well as Wales. Much enclosure had already occurred in eastern England. But over a large part of central England the open fields remained with vast arable areas and great tracts of common pasture. Here the transformation was to the modern chequer-board pattern of small, squarish fields enclosed by hedges or fences. It was a monotonous field pattern compared with the multi-coloured patchwork of the arable strips. Heathland and pastures too were transformed into corn fields. The changes were rapid. In most places enclosure occurred within a year or two of the parliament passing the necessary Act. In Scotland people were 'cleared' from the Highlands to make way for sheep. This resulted in a landscape of deserted farms and broken-down fences.

The industrial landscape began to evolve in the early eighteenth century. Hoskins describes it as 'a 'busy' landscape, full of detail and movement . . . not a massive conglomeration of factories and slums'. The move of some industries to factories led to the development of the modern industrial landscape. People moved first to the new mills which tended to be on the hillsides somewhat remote from their homes and then, as coal replaced water as the source of power, down to the valley bottoms. Hamlets and villages quickly clustered round both. Water power did not create smoke or dirt. Only when coal was used directly did towns become blackened and air and water polluted. Steam power led to larger concentrations of industries and of labourers needed to work them, preferably adjacent to canals or navigable rivers. This meant flatter sites where building costs were cheaper but poor sanitary conditions were exacerbated. The result, as Engels among others pointed out, was the 'zoning' of urban society with a movement of the better-off out of the town centres to the growing suburbs. Between the densely populated and polluted towns – de Tocqueville called them 'an assault upon the nostrils' and Sheffield was described in the 1830s as being 'poisoned in its own excrement' – lay miles of desolate countryside covered with the waste of mining, disused pit-shafts and stagnant pools, what Wordsworth called 'the barren wilderness'. This landscape was not confined to the industrial North and Midlands. Cornwall had its china-clay landscape with mountains of white sterile waste on which little would grow.

Roads, canals and railways transected the country with their aqueducts, viaducts, cuttings and embankments, locks, bridges and stations. Their impact on the landscape may have been less dramatic than the expansion of towns, at least in the long-term. John Ruskin may have seen them 'brutally amputating every hill on their way' but their impact was more human than physical. Over 100 000 people were displaced from their homes in London alone as a result of railway building and many crowded even closer to the city centres because they could not afford to travel to work on the railways that had evicted them.

3   The national dimensions

Between 1800 and 1850 the balance of Britain's population shifted from the rural to urban setting. In the 1851 census, for the first time, there were more people living in towns and cities than in villages and hamlets. However, in large parts of Wales and Scotland and much of Ireland the rural dimension remained central to most people's lives.

In 1800 the population of Wales was nearly 600 000. It was fairly evenly spread across the whole country with some concentration in the mining areas of the north and south. There was little urbanisation – in 1801 only thirteen towns had over 3000 inhabitants and only seven had over 5000. More than three-quarters of the working population worked in self-contained farming communities, and communications were poor. The first half of the nineteenth century witnessed rapid industrial growth in the southern counties of Wales. Population growth, either natural or through migration, reflected this economic expansion and the importance of agriculture to Wales' economic life began to decline. Farming, however, remained vital in rural areas both as a source of food and employment. Demand for farm tenancies remained high and it was labourers unable to get farms who migrated to the towns. Historians have distinguished between the cereal producing 'lowland zone' of the coastal fringe, much enclosed during the French Wars, and the pastoral farming of the 'highland zone'. But development was limited by land hunger and the ignorance of tenants about new techniques as well as by the cultural gap between the anglicised, Anglican and Tory landowners and the Welsh-speaking, Nonconformist tenants [7.14]. Wales exhibited the same characteristics as Ireland and, to a lesser extent Scotland, where – unlike England – there was little or no community of feeling between landlords and their tenants.[18]

In Ireland the Catholicism of the peasantry and the absenteeism of many Protestant landlords led to a similar cultural gap.[19] Discussion of the Irish economy has tended to centre on the Famine, with economic trends up to 1845 being seen in the light of the 'Great Hunger'. Though there were signs of tension within the Irish economy before 1845 the Famine came as an intense shock to most contemporaries. In 1760 Ireland imported corn but by 1815 it was exporting both grain and livestock. There was a tendency away from arable to pasture but demand from mainland Britain stimulated prices and continued to make grain production profitable. But it was the potato which increasingly came to dominate both Irish farming and diet. It is a high yield crop which can be used for fattening stock and restoring the soil, as well as for food. The widespread growing of the potato had two major consequences for Ireland. The cultivation of potatoes was intensive and allowed the increase in small holdings – by 1845 twenty-four per cent of all holdings were between one and five acres and a further forty per cent between five and fifteen acres. Potatoes were a cash crop which could provide sufficient income from a small farm for a family. Constraints upon early marriage were removed and the Irish population began to grow rapidly. By 1845 roughly two-thirds of the entire population of Ireland were dependent on the potato for their existence. No wonder that the disasters of the mid 1840s took such catastrophic proportions.

But just how prosperous was Irish farming before 1845? From about 1820 demand for Irish products fell – wheat, oats, barley, bacon, beef and mutton were all affected – and the tendency towards growing potatoes increased. Persistent sub-division, overcropping and undermanuring of soil contributed to this. Livestock prices fell less dramatically and perceptive landlords soon appreciated that urban growth and rising standards of living meant markets for Irish meat. In 1825 some 47 000 Irish cattle were exported, rising to 98 000 in 1835 and 202 000 by 1850.

Irish agriculture was still largely traditional in technique and landlords generally made little attempt at improvement. David Ricardo wrote that 'Ireland is an oppressed country – not oppressed by England but by the aristocracy which rules with a rod of iron within it.' But historians should not generalise about an alien landowning class concerned with maximising profits, exploiting a hapless tenantry with high rents and the ever-present threat of eviction, reinforced by the Ejectment Acts of 1816–19, in the years leading up to the Famine. In fact the Famine, because of its reduction of population, made consolidation more of a possibility. The Irish land problem of the pre-1846 period was not that of the late nineteenth century.

Agriculture did not make up the whole of the Irish economy. Historians have suggested recently that a 'dual economy' existed with a subsistence agrarian economy on which three-quarters of the population depended, characterised by introspection and barter, *and* a maritime economy existing mainly on the eastern coastal fringe from Belfast to Cork, with offshoots at Limerick and Galway. It was outward-looking with a cash economy and trade with England. Useful though this is the line of demarcation between these two economies was imprecise. In fact the maritime economy was perhaps more vulnerable to depressed economic trends than its agrarian counterpart and its development followed the booms and slumps of the mainland economy quite closely.

Before 1850 Ireland's economic development was hindered by an underdeveloped communications system. Railways spread slowly and only 578 kilometres of track were open by 1849. Dublin remained the financial capital but it was the Lagan valley and Belfast that dominated Ireland's Industrial Revolution. Linen was still largely a domestic industry and had long been manufactured. But by 1810 it was cotton that dominated textile production, employing 2000 people in Belfast alone. However, after 1815 and certainly after 1830 the pendulum swung towards factory-produced linen. This stimulated both a growth in engineering and an influx of people into Belfast. By 1841 the city had 75 000 inhabitants, and had become the leading port, exporting eight million pounds worth of goods, half of them linen. Wool and woollen goods were less centralised but nonetheless prosperous in the first half of the nineteenth century.

Scotland too had a 'dual economy' – the lowland and highland economies.[20] It also experienced a demographic revolution after 1750. Between 1755 and 1820 the Scottish population grew from 1.26 to 2.10 million. The focal point of this growth was in the lowland area with three out of five people living there by 1820. Though more people lived in towns – Edinburgh's population increased from 81 000 in 1801 to 138 000 twenty years later – as late as 1820 seventy per cent of people lived in rural communities. From the 1780s Scotland underwent both industrial and agrarian change which committed it, far more than either Wales or Ireland, to becoming a society in which rapid and accelerating change was a feature of life. As in England, old and new methods of production co-existed until well after 1850. The motive force for change in Scotland came largely from England – though James Watt was a Scot! – but the prosperity of the Scottish economy itself provided much of the internal strength for change. Capital and experience gained in the linen industry was easily transferred to cotton production. Glasgow's tobacco trade gave the exporting stimulus necessary for a growing economy. The expansion of the west coast cotton industry is clearly demonstrated in raw cotton imports via the River Clyde – 0.15 million pounds weight in 1770 to 7.5 million pounds in 1801 – and by the increase in yarn bought from Manchester and the Lancashire cotton mills. The powerloom was adopted less quickly than in England. In 1820 there were only 2000 powerlooms as compared to 50 000 handlooms. This can be explained by the fine cotton cloth produced in Scotland which machines could still not produce and by the reservoir of cheap labour. But even in Scotland the inexorable process of change was only slowed. Factories using steam power replaced water powered mills and better machines were developed. By 1850 the Scottish handworkers were superfluous and appallingly pauperised and depressed.

In farming, almost everything was borrowed from England. Ideas of rotation, new crops like rye-grass, clover, potatoes and turnips, methods of enclosure, owed much to the English improvers of the eighteenth century. But eventually methods like 'Lothian husbandry' were held in the same esteem and copied in England just as the Norfolk system had been earlier in Scotland. Scottish pioneers developed a threshing machine in 1786 and a horse-drawn reaper in 1826 and, more importantly, developed methods of field drainage which allowed a revolution on Britain's heavy clay soils. The problems of the Scottish Highlands were, Eric Richards argues, in the same category as Ireland's.[21] Clearances of tenants, mainly between 1780 and 1855, allowed commercial production of sheep. The traditional view is that the Clearances represented the end of the old clan system, the demolition of the old highland communities based upon kinship, and were the antithesis of the old paternalistic and communal social and economic system. Those who remained in the Highlands – many chose emigration – reverted to a subsistence economy, living in a vast rural slum, existing on potatoes. In reality they were the result of demographic and economic forces operating on a dependent and insecure society, beyond the control of local landowners who had little alternative but to respond to market forces.

In Wales, Ireland and Scotland, perhaps more than in England, historians have fired the myths first put forward by contemporaries. There may well have been widespread exploitation, discrimination on religious grounds, lack of understanding of the problems of many by the politically and economically dominant few. English influence or control may well have been alien. But it is important to appreciate the diversity of contemporary experience and the limited value of over-generalisation.

4 The English experience

This same variety of economic and social experience existed in England. As with lowland Scotland and to a lesser extent Wales and Ireland, it is important not to overestimate the distinction between town and country, city and village. Their relationship was fluid, based upon mutual need. For example, though industry became increasingly urbanised there were still important rural industries which, even if they did look to towns, were based in rural settings – the straw-plaiting industry round Luton used up large amounts of labour with almost half of the population of adjacent villages in some way associated with straw. Changes in technology, especially after 1820, led to the countryside becoming the reservoir of cheap labour for the towns [4.21], a process eased by the development of the railway system. But, this was not a one-way process. Urban workers often left the towns at harvest times and went into the countryside to help gather the crops. The wealthier sections of urban society moved out of the town centres into the surrounding villages which then grew into suburbs.

The idea of a 'dual economy' is too simple for the English economy. There certainly was a notion of the English economy as such – this is explicit in the writings of economists from Adam Smith to John Stuart Mill. But it is perhaps better to look at England as having regionalised economies based upon one or two major industries, with access to both local raw materials and national and international markets. Within the regions, employment was largely in the regional industries, or closely related ones, and contemporary perception of issues and reaction to them tended to be directly determined by regional expectations. These regions overlapped and were of approximately a hundred miles in diameter.[22] Two areas – Lancashire and London – will be considered in more detail.

The cotton industry is seen as central to the Industrial Revolution. It was highly regionalised. After Lancashire, the next most important centre of the cotton industry was based round Glasgow, employing less than one-twentieth of those working in the Lancashire industry. The reasons for this concentration are partly geographical – ease of access to raw cotton, climatic conditions, water and coal resources – and partly the change in circumstances that operated after 1780. By 1800 cotton production was centred round Manchester and by 1812 seven to eight per cent of Britain's Gross National Product (GNP) was accounted for by cotton. Within the region there was some functional specialisation. By 1850 cotton weaving became concentrated in the North and spinning in the South, separated by the upland Rossendale. The reasons for this are unclear though early specialisation, like that of Bolton in fine spinning, played a significant part. Cheap labour and improved rail access led to new weaving factories being set up in northern towns like Blackburn and Burnley.

Urban growth in this area was dominated by Manchester and Liverpool. By 1851 Manchester and neighbouring Salford contained 455 153 people compared to 25 000 in 1772. Much of this growth – which by 1850 left Manchester as a warehousing and servicing centre rather than as a factory city – was unplanned. Even so Manchester inspired both wonder and shock: Engels highlighted not its wealth but its social segregation. Liverpool too had grown rapidly, to nearly 400 000 in 1851, first upon the profits of slavery and, after 1790, on cotton. It too saw segregation made worse by the large number of Irish immigrants who made up almost a quarter of Liverpool's population in 1851. Its public health problems led to its pioneering appointment of a Medical Officer of Health in 1846.

It was London however, which exhibited an expansion that outstripped the experience of Derbyshire and Lancashire to such an extent that their rate of growth was less than the national average. London exerted an intense pressure on the surrounding counties and it sucked in people: by 1831 it accounted for eleven per cent of the population of England and Wales. By mid century a quarter of Britain's entire trade was conducted on the Thames. London's importance as a centre of 'manufacturing industry' is generally overlooked in this period. In fact London was the country's principal centre of production. But it was not production on the Lancashire model. London was a centre of small businesses. Small firms predominated: like silk weaving around Spitalfields in the East End, shoemaking, cabinet making, building and dockworking. In 1831 businesses using steam power were few. Most firms employed under a hundred men: Wigram & Green shipbuilders, employing 400 to 500 shipwrights and up to two hundred other workers, was an exception. But urban expansion brought with it an increase in slums – Seven Dials, Whitechapel, Bethnal Green – as well as major public health problems. The Thames was an open sewer.

The surrounding counties, as well as providing manpower, satisfied some of London's economic needs as well as being stimulated by them. The great markets of Covent Garden, Billingsgate and Smithfield predated this expansion but the produce of the surrounding districts, fish from the coast and cattle from Wales and Scotland were brought in increasing amounts to the metropolis.

There was considerable diversity of experience in regions where farming was the main activity. Though the economic and territorial dominance of the large farm was established by 1830 most farming was on a much smaller scale. The experience of Buckinghamshire was representative of most southern counties. In 1851, 1810 farms can be identified of which 872 were between one hundred and three hundred acres and 229 over three hundred acres with an average size of 179 acres. In Yorkshire, by contrast, seventy per cent of farms were under one hundred acres and in Lancashire and Cheshire the figure was ninety per cent. There were only 7771 farms in England in 1851 of over one thousand acres while some 142 358 farms were under one hundred acres.

Enclosure may have changed the landscape of many parts of rural England but its impact on life was ambiguous [1.3, 1.4, 2.3]. It did not lead initially to the lessening of labour demands since it brought more land under cultivation. Rural depopulation did not begin in earnest till the 1830s under the pressure of technological change. Rural poverty was to be found in areas like Hampshire and Dorset, where there was little enclosure and little industrial activity to absorb the surplus labour. The nature of a parish also influenced developments. 'Closed' parishes with one major landowner usually had small villages, lower poor rates and a process of hiring labour from surrounding parishes when necessary. Woburn in Bedfordshire, dominated as it was, and is, by the dukes of Bedford is a good example of a 'closed' parish. By contrast 'open' parishes saw no sole landowner with a monopoly over land. Villages tended to be large, ill-planned and poorly built. Leading inhabitants were often tradesmen and small builders and 'open' parishes often straggled into small towns losing much of their original connection with the land, especially if the railways came. For example, Eastwood in Nottingham, D. H. Lawrence's childhood home, lost its rural character once its coal deposits were exploited. 'Open' parishes were not just physically open but also open to entrepreneurial

exploitation and change in a way that parishes like Woburn were not.
It may be useful to consider the following questions when discussing the
way in which regions changed during this period.

(i)   Is the region clearly definable?
(ii) What is its physical and climatic structure?
(iii) What were the dominant industries and where were they located?
(iv) What was the regional structure of society – location of population,
      religion, employment/under-employment/unemployment?
(v)   What was the regional perception on particular issues – internal
      issues and issues external to the region?

It was the regionalised nature of Britain and the issues which were raised
in those regions that determined the political and social agenda in the first
half of the nineteenth century.

C   The nature of society

Between 1800 and 1850 it is possible to identify two dominant views
about the nature of British society: on the one hand there was a
paternalistic view, and on the other hand a view focused on the notion of
social class.[23]

I   Paternalism and deference

In 1800 economic, social and political power still lay with those who
owned or farmed land. Enclosure and other agricultural changes led to
some consolidation of land but the small farm remained widespread. This
landed society[24] was hierarchically graduated in a subtle way. At its apex
stood the great landowners. They formed an aristocratic elite, a kind of
'ruling class', who monopolised economic and political power. Their
income came increasingly from land rents, both for farming land and
building land in the expanding towns – and, if they were lucky, from
minerals found beneath their land. They were adaptable, if conservative,
in outlook. Beneath the landowners, the major social distinctions lay
between those who owned land or freeholders, and between those who
were tenants and those who worked for a wage. In reality these
distinctions were not that clearly defined: often freeholders were also
tenants, and wage-earners rented a small plot of land on which they grew
crops for self-consumption or the market. Wage-earners and small farmers
could also supplement their income by 'piece-work' for domestic
industries.
The underlying basis of this society was one of mutual and reciprocal

obligation within the hierarchical framework [5.6, 7.2]. People identified their place in society in relation to those above and below them and not by reference to those of the same social status. Deferential attitudes were due to those above and paternalistic attitudes to those below. It was a form of social organisation that, despite its obvious inequalities and injustices, was acceptable to the vast majority of people in England and Scotland where the landlord was usually of the same nationality and culture. This was less the case in Wales and hardly applied at all in Ireland where landlords were often from both an alien culture and religion.

Britain possessed a social structure characterised by many strata, each with a different measure of status and power and each with its own economic 'interests'. There was the landed interest, outlined above, but there were also employers and workers involved in industrial production (John Rule identified four main kinds of workers: artisans, miners, journeymen and house-based outworkers,[25]) financiers and entrepreneurs, and a growing number of factory workers. In 1800 the characteristic ideology was still a conservative one. 'Paternalism', in its broadest sense, governed not just relationships between landowner and labourer, and master and men, but existed at all levels [6.4, 6.5]. E. P. Thompson has pointed out that apprenticeship was more than induction into particular skills; it was also an immersion in the 'social experience or common wisdom of the community' and that can easily be extended to include agricultural workers. By these means, practices, norms and attitudes were reproduced through successive generations within the accepted framework of traditional customs and rights that made up the 'moral economy'.

But was there a 'consensus' view of society? Many of the disturbances in the latter years of the eighteenth and the early nineteenth century were directed as infringements of the 'moral economy' – low wages or high prices could provoke violent consumer responses, as in East Anglia in 1816 and 1822, especially when magistrates were unwilling to enforce old regulations for the corn trade [2.8(a)–(d)]. New technology in either an industrial or rural setting could lead to a job response, as the Luddite outbreaks [4.8–4.11] and the 'Captain Swing' riots [2.12(a)–(e)] showed. Responses were conservative in form, appealing to custom and paternalistic Tudor and Stuart legislation, and seeking to establish traditional practices [4.13–4.14]. The breaking down of that consensus was the result of economic changes, the expansion of towns which were generally outside the paternal net, changing religious observance (especially Methodism which broke the 'bond of dependency' between squire, parson and labourer), 'the abdication on the part of the governors' (as Thomas Carlyle termed it), and the dismantling of the protection of paternalistic legislation [4.5].

Despite this and the emergence of the class alternative, paternalism continued to possess currency. David Roberts provides the fullest analysis of paternalism in early Victorian society.[26] His approach is a broad one and has been subjected to some criticism for being conceptually confused. However, his model for paternalism is still the best starting point. The paternalist, he argues, saw society in the following way:

1 It should be **authoritarian**.

> The typical paternalist believed in capital punishment, whipping, severe game laws, summary justice for delinquents, strict laws defining the duties of servants and the imprisonment of seditious writers. He never doubted the sacred nature of paternal authority, whether exercised by magistrates . . . landlords . . . or by archdeacons

However, this was an authoritarianism tempered by common law and ancient liberties.

2 It should be **hierarchical**.

> At the heart of a paternalist's hierarchical outlook is a strong sense of the value of dependency, a sense that could not exist without those who are dependent having an unquestioned respect for their betters.

3 It should be **organic**.

> Paternalists believed in the body politic, one in which every part had an appointed and harmonious place. Whether a ploughman or a bishop, each individual had his function, his place, his protectors, his duties, his reciprocal obligations and his strong ties of dependency.

4 It should be **pluralistic**.

> Society consisted of many differing spheres, each with its own hierarchies, though each was part of a larger one.[27]

Within this social fabric the paternalist notion that 'property has its duties as well as its rights' was worked out. These duties fell into three main areas:

1 The duty to rule came directly from wealth and power. Paternalists owed protection to those of lower status and it was their duty 'to suppress crime, riot and disorder, to put to work the idle, to reprimand servants, to

tell bailiffs how to manage farms and to see that vagrants were expelled from the parish' [7.12].

2 Parallel to this was the duty of guidance, a firm moral superintendence: 'Paternal authorities know what is good for those dependent on them just as a father knows what is good for his children' [5.12, 5.13].

3 The third duty was helping the poor, not just benevolence but active assistance: 'Soup should be dispensed during periods of severe want, coal should be sold cheaply in frost-ridden January, cottages should be built and let at moderate rates'.[28]

Round these social assumptions and duties clustered many different attitudes:

1 That men of property and rank had managed society much better in the past – an inherently conservative and retrospective ethos.

2 An intense suspicion, Roberts goes so far as to call it 'hatred', of money since it was 'rootless, mobile, free of obligations, knowing no duty'.

3 A belief in the inevitability of poverty which could be blunted but never removed.

4 The moral and spiritual regeneration of society was the means to a more Christian and stable society, not legislation. Paternalists were sceptical of the value of legislation though some, like Oastler [5.16], Sadler and Shaftesbury, did support it.

5 'Morality should govern all relations, including economic ones': it was possible to identify a 'just' wage, a 'fair' price and a 'fair' rent, according to the rhetoric. In practice most paternalists were more level-headed and pragmatic.[29]

Roberts sums up paternalists as those,

> who believe that society can be best managed and social evils
> mitigated by men of authority, property and rank performing their
> respective duties towards those in their community who are bound to
> them by personal ties of dependency.[30]

This applies as much to industrialists like the Ashworths and Samuel Greg as to landowners and clergymen. Paternalism was the ethos not merely of continuity but also of nostalgia.

2 'Class', 'mass' and 'labour'

Just how many classes can historians identify in the early nineteenth century? What did contemporaries understand by 'class'? Was there a working class in 1800 or 1830 or 1850? Five main approaches have been used by historians when approaching 'class', according to R. S. Neale.[31] Three of them – the conventional 'three-class' model, the approach through 'class-consciousness' and the approach through contemporary perceptions – are seen by Neale as being methods used by most historians. The other two approaches – the 'two-class' Marxist model and its modification by constructing explicit sociological models – adopt a more interdisciplinary approach. Whatever model is used, the years since the publication of E. P. Thompson's *The Making of the English Working Class* in 1963 have been punctuated by an extensive 'class' debate. Yet in relation to the 'big' questions of when, where, how and why it has been surprisingly inconclusive.

Contemporaries noted that change was breaking down the basic tenets of paternalism. Disraeli wrote of 'Two nations; between whom there is no intercourse and no sympathy'. Elizabeth Gaskell said, 'I never lived in a place before where there were two sets of people always running each other down.'

This breakdown in the system of dependency had its origins in the eighteenth century. Thompson has argued that changing landownership and land-use did cause the fracturing of traditional social ties in the countryside, a process assisted by changing religious observance. This can also be seen in the urban expansion of the same period. But was it a 'class' response? Harold Perkin maintains that 'class was indeed latent in the 18th century'. In 1978 Thompson argued, paradoxically, that eighteenth-century English society had class struggle without class. He identified a traditional, classless popular culture that was rebellious and resisted the inroads of market forces and capitalist relationships within a hierarchical framework. Perkin then argued that, as a result of industrialisation and particularly urban growth, a class society emerged between 1789 and 1833 and, more precisely, between 1815 and 1820. To him class is characterised 'by class feeling, that is, by the existence of vertical antagonisms between a small number of horizontal groups, each based on a common source of income'.[32]

But the old society was not destroyed by these class antagonisms. Reforms made by established institutions like Parliament resulted in social conflict being contained. Compromise was a central reason for the persistence of the older social values and structures. A mature class society, Perkin maintains, is not marked by the violence of an immature one. Each class developed its own 'ideal' and by 1850 it was possible to identify three major classes each with their own ideal: the entrepreneurial ideal of the middle class, the working class ideal and the aristocratic ideal based respectively upon profits, wages and rent. The 'struggle between ideals' was 'not so much that the ruling class imposes its ideal upon the rest, but that the class which manages to impose its ideal upon the rest becomes the ruling class'.[33] In Perkin's model the mature class society that emerged, despite the difference that existed between classes, was not marked by overt conflict but by tacit agreement and co-existence under the successful entrepreneurial ideal.

E. P. Thompson also maintains that class experience was largely the result of productive relations into which people entered. But for him the essence of class lay not in income or work but in 'class consciousness', the product of contemporary perceptions of capital and labour, exploiter and exploited. Thompson's is a two-class model:

> In the years between 1780 and 1832 most English working people came to feel an identity of interests as between themselves and as against their rulers and employers . . . the working class presence was, in 1832, the most significant factor in British political life.[34]

John Foster also considers class consciousness in the two-class Marxist framework though his central theme is 'the development and decline of a revolutionary class consciousness in the second quarter of the century.'[35] Concentrating on Oldham, a Lancashire cotton-spinning town, he argues that the working population were at first 'labour conscious', with improvements in the price of their own labour taking over from consumer prices as their main occupation. 'Class consciousness' then developed where industrial problems became politicised, as in the 1830s and 1840s, and where workers were inclined to revolutionary ideas and practices. Finally the working population came to a 'liberalised consciousness' by which the bourgeoisie, aided by economic prosperity, was able to attach important sections of the working population to a consensus ideology.

But there are other explanations. J. R. Vincent, using poll books to analyse political behaviour, concludes that voting behaviour was not determined by economic issues.[36] This may be applicable to the six per cent of the population who could vote in the 1840s, but it does not really deal with the class perceptions of the unenfranchised whom Thompson and Foster have written about. Iowerth Prothero has examined the artisans who were at the upper end of the labouring population.[37] He found that in those trades with traditional organisation and practices the workers were conscious of the value of their skills and the product of their labour. They did not conceive themselves as a class in conflict with their employers nor with the middle class generally. But they were opposed to the 'unacceptable face of capitalism' which they believed downvalued their skills and products and which attacked both their notion of respectability and independence.

In this emphasis on perception and consciousness, organisation often takes second place. In Craig Calhoun's recent study[38] the concept of 'community' has been used as a means of identifying those social organisations which determined social action. He concludes that traditional communities were the foundation for radical collective action and that they were the crucial bond unifying workers for collective action – he cites Luddism and the Pentridge Rising as examples of this. In fact it was collective action within the framework of the 'moral economy' – not class but 'populist' action – with the nature of the action determined by the nature of the threat to the communities. The working class that did eventually emerge was, according to Calhoun, not revolutionary but reformist, concerned with modifying the existing social, economic and political structure rather than creating a new one.

Even the conclusions that can be reached from the 'class' debate are tendentious:

1 By 1850 it is possible to identify a middle class with clearly defined 'consciousness' based upon the notions of respectability and self-help and with a strong organisational base. That 'consciousness' had percolated down and reinforced traditional 'artisan' views.

2 There were important distinctions within the working population based upon the rural/urban, agricultural/industrial, skilled/unskilled, technologically obsolete/innovative differences. These distinctions, a consequence of employment and geography, helped to determine attitudes and perception.

3 It is possible to identify forms of 'class-consciousness' among the working population. But they did not form a unified whole and found themselves in a somewhat ambiguous relationship with the more homogeneous middle class ideology. There were certainly some attempts to form national organisations for the working population but these lacked coherence. Community, locality and region played a far more important role.

4 The nature of action among the working population was determined largely by consumer interests – the price of food, level of employment, etc. – and by the unwillingness of the majority of working people to pursue actively a programme of social change outside the existing social, economic and political environment. The threat of revolution was a tactic in this process but never a likely eventuality. The distinction between those working people who wanted change through evolution and revolution is central to explaining different 'class' attitudes.

5 It is difficult to identify a coherent working class by 1850 in terms both of consciousness and organisation at a *national* level.

Perceptions of society were paralleled by changes in the idea of work or 'labour'. In the pre-industrial period 'labour' was based upon the following:

1 The seasons (not surprisingly, in an economy in which farming played such a central part).

2 The home, but only to a certain extent. The family was not only a social unit but an economic one as well.

3 More than just wages. Workers often had access to the land as a means of subsistence – in fact the production of food took precedence over manufacturing and other activities at certain times of the year.

4 A relationship between employer and worker that was highly personal and paternalistic in character [7.2].

5 A more flexible economic structure, since it was based upon human effort rather than the inexhaustible effort of machines – workers could labour when they chose to or when necessary, though within a tight customal framework.

The development of an industrial economy led to fundamental shifts in the nature of 'labour'. Firstly, labour became the labour of the 'proletariat' who had no source of income other than the cash wages received for their work. This move to the 'cash nexus' marked a change from the much more complex relationship in both social and human terms that characterised the pre-industrial period [7.15–7.19].

Secondly, industrial labour, especially factory-working, imposed a regularity, a routine, which Engels called 'a tyranny' quite unlike pre-industrial rhythms. The pace of life was set not by people's physical endurance but by the pace of the machine. Workers were paid to make sure that their tasks were done efficiently – they were paid to be on time, alert and reliable, hence the seeming harshness of many factory rules.

Thirdly, 'labour' increasingly took place in an urban environment. It was this, as much as anything, which was responsible for the development of class feeling and eventually class organisation. Emphasis has been placed upon the idea of 'mass' in the following ways:

(i) physical 'massing' in towns;

(ii) economic 'massing' in factories characterised by 'mass' production;

(iii) eventually political 'massing' in an organised and self-organising class structure symbolised by the 'mass meeting.'[39]

Finally, the Christian work ethic which underpinned labour in the pre-industrial period was modified and secularised in the idea of 'self-help', which extolled the virtues of good, hard-working and loyal workers.

It is possible to argue that between 1800 and 1850 there were *three* rather than two views of society being debated by contemporaries. On the one hand there was the paternalistic model based upon hierarchical principles, with implicit inequalities but reciprocal obligations, created by a pre-industrial economic environment. On the other hand there were two class models. The 'revolutionary' class model was based upon horizontal social groupings, with co-operation as the motive force. There was antagonism or class conflict between them and at its heart was a critique of industrial capitalism. The 'evolutionary' class model too was based upon horizontal groupings but with individual competitiveness at its core within the actual industrial and urban environment. In this model, change occurred as a result of negotiation on specific issues to make the existing system more fair and consensual in character. These ideas can be seen in the diagram.

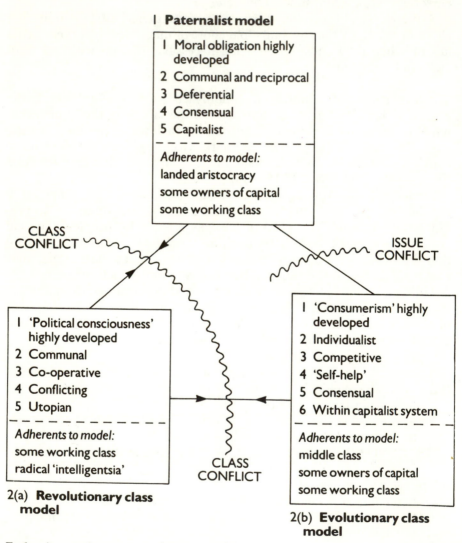

I Paternalist model

I Moral obligation highly developed
2 Communal and reciprocal
3 Deferential
4 Consensual
5 Capitalist

Adherents to model:
landed aristocracy
some owners of capital
some working class

CLASS CONFLICT

ISSUE CONFLICT

I 'Political consciousness' highly developed
2 Communal
3 Co-operative
4 Conflicting
5 Utopian

Adherents to model:
some working class
radical 'intelligentsia'

2(a) **Revolutionary class model**

CLASS CONFLICT

I 'Consumerism' highly developed
2 Individualist
3 Competitive
4 'Self-help'
5 Consensual
6 Within capitalist system

Adherents to model:
middle class
some owners of capital
some working class

2(b) **Evolutionary class model**

Early nineteenth-century society – a model

D   Authority, resistance and reform

I   The nature of authority

Authority is the right to act rather than the power to act. It may be coupled with power and therefore capable of being upheld, or it may be without power and ignored. Authority may also be held *de jure* and legitimated through the 'rule of law'. However, one of the most important powers that upholds authority is the power of people's belief in it. Marxists perceive the state as the symbol of the economic and political dominance of the 'ruling class'. It will be used to uphold that dominance through control of the instruments of coercion. This control is seen as essential to maintaining order and social stability. But without 'moral' authority – that is, the willingness of the population to obey the state passively if not actively – no developing state could survive for any length of time. Revolution did not occur in Britain between 1790 and 1850 because *most* people were willing to support a state which eventually showed itself willing to adapt to changing social needs most of the time.

Before and during the first part of the Industrial Revolution, authority was maintained by the existence of the paternalist social structure and the protection this afforded to those at the lower levels of society. Sometimes because of a breakdown in the perceived 'moral economy' this was put under stress. On those occasions the Riot Act could be read, and local volunteers, militia and even regular troops called upon. These reinforced the local magistracy who through their courts were able to deal with infringements of the law, with particular severity in the case of attacks on property.[40] The Church of England, through its close links with the local squire, was able to exert spiritual pressure. Such was the power of the pulpit. Many clergymen were also magistrates and took an active part in putting down unrest [see Chapter 2].

The changes in the economy and especially the expansion of an urban society outside the existing system of dependency led to pressure on authority. Volunteers were still used, though the reaction of the yeomanry at Peterloo in 1819 led to a serious examination of their role. R. J. Morris comments that 'the authorities realised that the presence of the yeomanry exacerbated class feeling rather than restoring social peace'.[41]

Regular troops were used. It is said that more troops were used to deal with Luddism than the Duke of Wellington had at his disposal in Spain. Regular troops were used to keep order during the reform agitations of 1815–19 and 1830–2, but it was during the early stages of Chartism, and especially in 1839 and 1840, that the authorities skilfully deployed their forces. Local magistrates may have wanted strong measures, but a low profile policy interspersed occasionally with judicious shows of strength, as practised by General Napier, proved highly successful. Discussions with Chartist leaders proved far more valuable than confrontation. Troops could be held back to allow Chartist rioters to run out of steam. The initiative always lay with the authorities.

The most important change in the character of authority was the introduction of an organised police force in London in 1829, in the municipal towns after 1836 and in the counties after 1839.⁴² Their introduction was opposed in many communities and it was not until the 1850s that they gained acceptance – if not popularity. But in July 1839 *The Times* could write that the Whig government had created conditions in which life and property had to be protected 'by an apparatus which we have no question will be very injurious to public and general liberty and the free expression of opinion'.

Coercion and the 'rule of law' are but two facets of authority, and social systems do not normally rely on force alone. This has led to historians paying increasing attention to the concept of 'hegemony' developed by the Italian Marxist, Antonio Gramsci.⁴³ 'Hegemony' means that the 'ruling class' has succeeded in persuading the rest of society to accept its own moral, political and cultural values. In successful cases, Gramsci argued, this involved the minimum use of force though it does imply an element of direction and cultural control. He maintained that the 1830s and 1840s brought a crisis of hegemony. On the one hand more effective coercive institutions like the police force and the new Poor Law [see Chapter 5] were introduced. But, on the other hand, there was an acceptance of the need for concessions to the middle class and for the representation of the economic interests of skilled workers through the development of their own organisations, especially trade unions, co-operative and friendly societies. These organisations were autonomous, and even though some challenged the basic assumptions of the capitalist system they were not a direct threat to the 'ruling class'.

Religion and education [see Chapter 6] played a central part in the maintenance of hegemony, hence the concern over the findings of the Religious Census of 1851 and the contemporary debate over state funding of education. From the 1790s there was a concerted increase in the religious and educational activities of middle and ruling classes – the conservative impact of Wesleyan Methodism with its emphasis on 'proper' education [6.9–6.13], the growth of Sunday schools, the emergence of the Temperance movement, the work of Hannah More and the Bible and Tract Societies [6.14], government financing of an Anglican urban church-building programme after 1818 and grants to the educational societies after 1833. The emphasis was upon education as a means of social discipline [6.1, 6.2, 7.6]. These attempts to influence behaviour and ideals in particular directions can be seen as 'cultural aggression'. Added to this were well-calculated concessions which divided opinion and convinced many working people that their interests were better served by the existing social ethos.

The 1851 Religious Census showed how far religious observance had ceased to be considered necessary [**6.20(a)–(c)**]. Although decline and fall is the model favoured by most historians of nineteenth-century religion it does have some puzzling features. There was the inventiveness and energy of many churchmen but there was also their apparent ineffectiveness. The commitment, intelligence and money poured into religious enterprise was probably greater than ever before. So why was decline not halted? Is the growth of urban life outside the traditional hegemony of the Church a sufficient answer to the question?

Social control and acceptance of the existing dominant ideology exerted through education, the Churches, the societies for moral improvement and by sections of the working population, were far more insidious and effective than the use of force. Concession was much easier than confrontation as a way of re-establishing consensus. The adaptability of the ruling class meant that it was able to maintain its authority largely intact against those threatening class warfare.

2 Resistance to change

Changes, either proposed or actual, alter established norms of social and economic organisation. Individual livelihood and employment may be threatened. Vague notions of custom may be infringed, the 'moral economy' challenged. In the early nineteenth century responses were often based upon 'consumer' principles, and protest often took the form of riot. E. J. Hobsbawm has seen this as an early form of 'collective bargaining'. The demand was for certain specific grievances to be remedied – that prices, particularly of bread, should be reduced, machines removed, enclosures pulled down.[44] Failure to achieve this was generally followed by riots, attacks on property and occasionally on people though usually this only went so far as symbolic burning in effigy. Justice offended, direct action followed. Rioters were only acting to restore what was traditionally theirs. E. P. Thompson comments that 'an outrage to these moral assumptions, quite as much as actual deprivation, was the usual occasion for direct action'.[45]

The commonest and perhaps clearest kind of action based upon this sense of legitimation were food riots.[46] They were in the main the direct collective action of town artisans and non-agricultural labourers, though in the 1816 East Anglian riots farm labourers were involved as well [**2.10**]. Food-rioting was a strategy employed by urban and industrial workers in defence of their living standards and was particularly directed against those exporting grain either out of the country or the region. In the late eighteenth and first half of the nineteenth century the focal points for rioting moved northwards and westwards, a result of the shift in population, which put considerable strain upon local marketing systems. This can be seen in the 1847 food riots in north-east Scotland where agrarian changes had widened the productive capacity of the region. Wheat production had expanded and there had been a revolution in herring fishing. Changing occupational needs led to the increase of fishermen, curers and other artisans who supported themselves with small potato plots. The failure of this crop in 1846 and 1847 led to increased demands for other staple foodstuffs, especially wheat. The clash was between the fishermen and the merchants or corn dealers who believed in a market economy and were unwilling to bend to what the fishermen saw as their social responsibility in times of distress. Parallel protests occurred in Cornwall and at St Helier, on Jersey. The end of rioting in the three areas was the result of improved prospects in employment, weather and fishing – not a decline in prices.

Apart from the 1847 riots the main period of activity was between 1802 and 1818, especially in the years 1810–13 and 1816–18. Again, these riots were related to food shortages and high prices. In 1812 action spread from the tinners of Cornwall, through Bristol, to the industrial areas of Lancashire, north-east Cheshire and the West Riding of Yorkshire. Some outbreaks occurred in Scotland but none in Wales. In 1816–18, though towns and industrial areas were the loci of food protests, there were important outbreaks in the Fens [2.11].

Food-rioting became less important in the nineteenth century. It is interesting to consider why. Some historians see this as a result of changes in the nature of economic activity. In growth industries like coal, iron and textiles the shift towards wage bargaining came at the end of the eighteenth century. The cyclical nature of the industrial economy and the incidence of slump was not directly related to bad harvests. But the introduction of wage-cutting, backed up by troops, was increasingly used after 1800. In this situation workers were more concerned with maintaining their wages than with prices alone. Lower grain prices between 1816 and 1846, the development of the railway system, developments in the retail and wholesale trade: all these added to the weakness in the bargaining position of many industrial workers assisted in bringing the food-rioting to an end.

In industrial areas machine-breaking was a traditional way of express-ing protest. The destruction of new technology was a symbolic as well as a practical reassertion of traditional techniques. The most widespread period of machine-breaking was between 1811 and 1816 and is usually called

Luddism.[47] In the hosiery and lace-making areas of Nottinghamshire, Derbyshire and Leicester, frames were broken in 1812, 1814 and 1816 [4.7, 4.8]. In 1812 croppers of woollen cloth broke new shearing frames in Yorkshire and in Lancashire new powerloom mills were attacked. In fact the aims of the attackers in the three areas were different. In Nottinghamshire frames were broken, not because they caused unemployment, but because of wage reductions or employers using unapprenticed workers or paying 'truck'. In Yorkshire [4.11] machines were attacked because croppers saw them as leading to unemployment and the destruction of their privileged positions as the aristocracy of West Riding woollen workers. In Lancashire [4.9] handloom weavers were supported by other workers. Here it was not the actual machines (which did not become widespread till the 1820s) that led to frame-breaking but the *fear* of machines which in some way symbolised distress.

Although machine-breaking persisted it became increasingly sporadic as did other traditional forms of industrial protest. Resistance to change took other forms. From 1815 to 1850 economic distress led to strikes [4.12–4.18] and to a resurgence of demands for radical political reform. These disturbances were increasingly based in the growing industrial centres: in 1832, for example, they were in London and Birmingham in particular, but violent riots also occurred in Derby, Nottingham and Bristol. The end of Chartism led to public protest becoming more muted. Negotiation and bargaining replaced much direct action. Yet passions could still be aroused – Catholic versus Protestant in Stockport in 1852, riots over Sunday trading in Hyde Park in 1855.

In rural areas traditional methods of resisting change remained important for longer.[48] Between 1815 and 1831 there were widespread outbursts of agrarian protest caused by falling wages, under-employment and the threat of machines. This protest was more keenly felt when there were no urban centres to soak up the surplus population [1.11, 1.12]. But in 1816 it was not just farm labourers who were involved in the 'Bread and Blood' riots – one in three arrested were artisans or small tradesmen. There was a diversity of demand: in the Fens this was a reflection of a variety of problems, from the Poor Law to drainage and enclosure; in Norfolk demands for higher wages and attacks on the use of the mole plough were more important. By contrast, the disturbances in 1822 were all protests by farm labourers in the Diss and Eye areas of Norfolk. In 1816 attacks on machines were largely symbolic, but in 1822 it became a campaign to sweep them away. The 'Captain Swing' riots of 1830 were far more widespread[49] but they too demonstrated regional diversity – new machinery, the Poor Law, high prices and low wages played different parts. These riots were rapidly and fairly easily suppressed and draconian sentences meted out [2.12(a)–(e)]. But these retributive measures did not destroy the labourer's will to resist, as historians once believed. There was widespread protest against the introduction of the new Poor Law throughout southern England [5.15(a)–(c)].

The old paternalist framework, which allowed collective action as a legitimate means of expressing grievances, had been dismantled, but labourers still clung to the archaic values of that society [2.11(a)–(d)]. Threatening letters and arson attacks increased. Between 1840 and 1845 there were 196 arson attacks in Suffolk and sheep-stealing and egg-stealing also increased. In Wales there was widespread resistance to the collection of debts, removal of squatters and the enclosure of wastes and commons, in the process of which gentry and government officials were assaulted and their homes fired. Though the turnpikes played a major part in the Rebecca Protests of 1839–44, the causes were far more complex – people complained of church-rates, tithes, high rents, the poor laws, insensitive agents and the Anglican magistracy. In Ireland, robbery of arms, forcible possession of property, armed assembly, attacks on houses, land and policemen played a far more important part than in Britain.

There was considerable resistance to change throughout Britain and Ireland between 1800 and 1850 but the face of protest did begin to change. The following conclusions are possible:

1 Protesters selected their targets carefully even though much of this protest was spontaneous, unstructured and largely unorganised.

2 The outlook of many protesters was backward-looking – redress of grievances was sought not through political reform but through a restoration of older, 'golden', happier times.

3 The location of property and the nature of protest both, however, changed.

By the 1850s the volume of protest throughout Britain and Ireland was in decline and the tendency was for such protest as there was to be centred not in the countryside but in the towns. Only in the southern counties of Ireland and parts of Scotland did the face of rural protest and rural resistance to change remain largely unaltered.

3   The need for reform

By 1850 the authorities had been very successful in controlling protests against industrial change and the demands of the working population for political reform. This had been achieved by judicious use of coercion, apt concession on fundamentals and some social reform. By 1850 the revolutionary thread had evaporated and the 'liberalised hegemony' of Victorian Britain had been established.

Was reform actually necessary in the first half of the nineteenth century? Were conditions really worse than in the last half of the eighteenth century? Industrial and particularly urban growth had increased the *scale* of the problem. Yet many of the social evils pre-date 1800 [3.5]. Poverty, crime, living and working conditions, the other iniquities of the economic, social and political condition had been debated and in some cases legislated for. The difficulty was that legislation like the Elizabethan Poor Law was designed for a traditional, rural, paternalistic society rather than a dynamic urban one. The strong paternalist strand in statutes on wages, prices and apprentices was but one aspect of the notion of the 'moral economy' which the classical economists attacked [5.5]. By 1820 much of this protection had been repealed and it had not been replaced by legislation appropriate to the changed environment.

Government was faced by a problem-ridden urban and industrial society and from the 1820s onwards a series of changes took place in the way this was approached.[50] The origins of the resulting reforms varied. In some cases, like the penal reforms of the 1820s, they originated within the sphere of government. But in others they were a response to pressure from outside, often middle-class, reformers with or without the support of the working population. The motives behind reform are also important. Was the motive social control? Improvement in conditions? Removal of abuse? Concessions? Despite the debate on the proper role of government[51] reforms fell into the following broad categories.

1 Reforms designed to remove obvious and unacceptable abuses within institutions – penal and legal reform from the 1820s, the limited reform of the franchise in 1832, the change in the status of the Church of England after 1828–9 and the establishment of the Ecclesiastical Commission in 1835.

2 Reforms designed to ameliorate living and working conditions – factory reform dating from the Health and Morals of Apprentices Act of 1802 through to the legislation of 1850 and 1853 that established the ten-hour day in textiles, the Mines Act of 1842, local initiatives on public health in the 1840s, which led to the 1848 Public Health Act.

3 Reforms designed to control the spiralling expense of dealing with the poor – the Poor Law (Amendment) Act of 1834.

4 The extension of state involvement in education from the 1830s.

The extent to which these reforms affected working people varied. Workers in mining were protected to a limited extent and an inspectorate ensured that in the textile industries the law was observed. But railway navvies were unprotected despite the Woodhead Scandal and the 1846 Select Committee report which, at Edwin Chadwick's recommendation, suggested that employers should pay compensation in the case of accidents. Handloom weavers and other outworkers received no legislative help, and neither did agricultural labourers. But even these limited

reforms were bitterly opposed. Reforms restricted property rights, individual liberty and economic profitability. Factory owners objected to the
legislation of the 1830s and 1840s but so did factory workers, because
reducing child labour reduced family incomes [3.4(a) and (b)]. The right to
defend long hours and squalid conditions was not the prerogative of the
employers and houseowners alone. Not till the 1870s did substantial and
enforceable legislation begin to deal with many of the problems of modern
industrial society.

Did these reforms strengthen the position of the establishment?
Anthony Brundage sees the 1834 Poor Law (Amendment) Act as the
culmination of centuries of shaping the Poor Laws to the needs of the
landed interest.[52] He rejects the view that the Act represented applied
Benthamism: 'Its purpose and result were to reorganise and strengthen the
power of the country's traditional leaders over their localities.'[53] He
maintains that between 1832 and 1839 it was 'indeed effective in
restoring social cohesion and . . . discipline and lowering the rates, though
not without some violent confrontations with the poor. This restoration
was due almost entirely to the effectiveness of the new boards of guardians,
rather than to the central commission or the operation of such doctrinaire
prescriptions as the workhouse.'[54] The Act did not interfere with paternalistic direction but strengthened it by making the operation of the Poor Law
a corporate activity for a district by a board composed of leading
landowners and farmers [5.12, 5.13]. Viewed in this context the use of 'new'
to describe the Poor Law after 1834 may need to be revised [see Chapter 5].
In urban areas too this political dimension was evident.[55] Charles Mott, an
Assistant Poor Law Commissioner, wrote in August 1841, 'Political party
feeling prevails to a mischievous extent at Leeds, the parties are nearly
balanced and it is scarcely possible to take any step . . . without exciting
strong party feeling.' Attacks on the Poor Law by Tories and Radicals alike
in urban areas [5.16, 5.17] in the 1830s were upon the inhumanity of its
treatment of already depressed workers. In Leicester, for example, the
Tories supported the framework knitters and, in true paternalist fashion,
reminded them that their true friends still cared for their plight.

The position of the establishment was strengthened by political reform.
The 1832 Reform Act may have extended the vote but it did so in a
circumspect manner.[56] The 'concessions' were to the urban middle class
and in rural areas the power of the landowner could well have been
increased.[57] The Chandos clause seems to have helped the Tories in the
counties though its effects were seldom decisive. Plenty of freeholders were
just as dependent on Tory landowners as any tenant-at-will. Where
county constituencies were uncontested – sixty per cent were uncontested
in 1847 – and landowners agreed on candidates, the 1832 Act was
irrelevant. Even so, few of the new voters wanted to challenge the landed

aristocracy. The middle class remained deferential within limits. The Act had not dethroned land and made industry supreme as Alexander Baring suggested.

The reforms of the first half of the nineteenth century were certainly necessary. They attempted to reduce social problems and tensions but had little real understanding of either their causes or scale [5.8, 5.14]. They were generally either permissive or specific in their field of application and met with limited success. The motives underlying reform were largely conservative and paternalist in tone, not surprising given the composition of parliament. They implied social control but hardly prevented revolution. They implied change, but change within a framework of continuity, a gradualism in which dynamic innovation never figured.

E   Conclusion

The idea of 'change' has dominated much writing on the early nineteenth century. It was taken further by the later Victorians in the ideology of progress. Though valuable in explaining the dramatic, revolutionary transformation, this emphasis has led to the idea of 'continuity' being either neglected or undervalued. Deferential attitudes, behaviour and work patterns were centrally linked to the legitimation of social hierarchy. They allowed power relations to be converted into moral ones and could ensure the stability of a hierarchy threatened by unstable and coercive class relationships. The hegemony of employers extended beyond the place of work in both rural and urban settings.[58] Deference remained strong because family and community did much to underpin it and the sense of mutual constraints beyond which people could not trespass retained their importance. But 'paternalism had to deliver the economic goods.'[59] Threats to jobs from new technology, the use of coercion and a falling level of economic well-being, as well as a growing sense of national economic unity, could all threaten the mechanisms of paternalism. But it was not until the economic crises of the 1870s and 1880s that the deferential mould was finally shattered and a fully class-conscious and class-organised society finally emerged.

Modes of production do co-exist. People can simultaneously live in different time-scales holding different values, believing different things, and having different priorities. At one moment in the early nineteenth century people could be living in the world of highly-skilled workers in a factory firm, while others could be tramping after sheep across the moors in a world whose mores were fixed by archaic customs. Yet they could be members of the same family.

References

1 J. F. C. Harrison, *The Common People*, 1984, p. 211
2 E. P. Thompson, 'Time and Work-Discipline', *Past and Present*, Dec. 1967, pp. 93–4
3 For useful discussions of this historiographical problem see M. W. Flinn, *Origins of the Industrial Revolution*, Longman, 1972, pp. 1–11, and the collection of essays by R. M. Hartwell, *The Industrial Revolution*, 1971, especially 'Interpretations of the Industrial Revolution in England', pp. 81–105
4 E. H. Carr, *What is History?*, 1964, p. 22
5 G. R. Elton, *The Practice of History*, Fontana, 1969, p. 20
6 J. H. Hexter, *The History Primer*, 1971
7 For a detailed discussion of the full variety of primary material it is perhaps best to turn to local history: W. B. Stephens, *Sources for English Local History*, Manchester, 1976 and A. Rogers, *Approaches to Local History*, Longman, 1977
8 E. Richards, *A History of the Highland Clearances*, vol. 1, Croom Helm, 1982, preface, pp. ii–iii
9 W. G. Hoskins, *The Making of the English Landscape*, Penguin, 1970, preface
10 *Ibid.*
11 J. W. Miller, *The Philosophy of History with Reflections and Aphorisms*, 1982, p. 187
12 M. I. Thomis, *Responses to Industrialisation*, David and Charles, 1976, Chapter 5, especially pp. 116–8
13 Of the many books on the British economy in this period, those by P. Mathias, *The First Industrial Nation*, 2nd ed, 1983; P. Deane, *The First Industrial Revolution*, 2nd ed., CUP, 1982; P. F. Speed, *The Growth of the British Economy 1700–1850*, Wheaton, 1980 are most useful
14 On population growth see N. L. Tranter, *Population Since the Industrial Revolution*, 1973; and M. W. Flinn, *British Population Growth 1700–1850*, 1970; and N. L. Tranter, *Population and Society 1750–1940*, Longman, 1985.
15 Agricultural change is best approached through J. Addy, *The Agrarian Revolution*, Longman, 1972; J. D. Chambers and G. E. Mingay, *The Agricultural Revolution 1750–1880*, 1966; and G. E. Mingay, *Rural Life in Victorian England*, Fontana, 1980
16 On the Industrial Revolution T. S. Ashton, *The Industrial Revolution 1760–1830*, OUP, 1955 is a readable though somewhat dated starting point but can be read alongside A. Briggs, *Iron Bridge to Crystal Palace – impact and images of the Industrial Revolution*, 1979
17 W. G. Hoskins, *The Making of the English Landscape*, Penguin, 1970, is still the best starting point

18   On developments in Wales see D. Williams, *A History of Modern Wales*, 2nd edn, 1977; G. E. Jones, *Modern Wales*, CUP, 1984; and D. W. Howell, *Land and People in Nineteenth Century Wales*, 1978

19   L. M. Cullen, *An Economic History of Ireland since 1660*, 1972; and F. S. L. Lyons, *Ireland Since the Famine*, 1971

20   On Scotland the most useful approach is through T. C. Smout, *A History of the Scottish People 1560–1830*, 1972

21   E. Richards, *A History of the Highland Clearances*, two vols, Croom Helm, 1982, 1986

22   For the nineteenth-century economy see F. Crouzet, *The Victorian Economy*, 1982; P. J. Perry, *A Geography of 19th Century Britain*, 1975; and the classic statement in J. Clapham, *An Economic History of Modern Britain, Volume 1*, CUP, 1926

23   The literature on the development of nineteenth-century society is voluminous. But the following are seminal: E. H. Hunt, *British Labour History 1815–1914*, 1981; R. J. Morris, *Class and Class Consciousness in the Industrial Revolution*, 1980; R. S. Neale, *Class in English History 1680–1850*, Blackwell, 1981; and the collection of papers by various writers which R. S. Neale edited, *History and Class*, Blackwell, 1983; H. Perkin, *The Origins of Modern English Society 1780–1880*, 1969; and for the committed reader, E. P. Thompson's magisterial, *The Making of the English Working Class*, 1963. Peter Calvert, *The Concept of Class*, 1983, is an approachable study of the nature of 'class'. By contrast paternalism has been less studied though G. Kitson Clark, *The Making of Victorian England*, 1970, is a good starting point to be followed up by D. Roberts, *Paternalism in Early Victorian England*, 1979 and J. C. D. Clark, *English Society 1688–1832*, CUP, 1985

24   See G. E. Mingay, *Landed Society in the Eighteenth Century*, 1963; R. Porter, *British Society in the Eighteenth Century*, Penguin, 1982; and F. M. L. Thompson, *Landed Society in the Nineteenth Century*, 1963

25   J. Rule, *The Experience of Labour in the Eighteenth Century Industry*, Croom Helm 1981, especially pp. 11–48 and 194–216

26   D. Roberts, *Paternalism in Early Victorian England*, 1979, pp. 2–10

27   *Ibid.* pp. 2–4

28   *Ibid.*, pp. 4–6

29   *Ibid.*, pp. 6–8

30   *Ibid.*, p. 8

31   R. S. Neale, *Class in English History 1680–1850*, Blackwell, 1981

32   H. Perkin, *The Origins of Modern English Society 1780–1880*, 1969, p. 176

33   *Ibid.*, p. 271

34   E. P. Thompson, *The Making of the English Working Class*, 1963, pp. 11–12

35   J. Foster, *Class Struggle and the Industrial Revolution*, 1974, p. 2

36   J. R. Vincent, Pollbooks, *How Victorians Voted*, 1967

37   I. Prothero, *Artisans and Politics in Early Nineteenth Century London*, 1979

38 C. Calhoun, *The Question of Class Struggle*, Blackwell, 1982

39 For a fuller discussion of 'mass' see Raymond Williams, *Culture and Society*, Penguin, 1961, and his *Keywords*, 1976, pp. 158–163

40 See D. Hay *el al.*, *Albion's Fatal Tree*, 1975, pp. 17–64, 189–344

41 R. J. Morris, *Class and Class Consciousness in English History 1780–1850*, 1980, p. 57

42 T. A. Critchley, *A History of Police in England and Wales*, 1978 edn, especially Chapters 2, 3 and 4

43 Useful introduction to 'hegemony' can be found in J. Joll, *Gramsci*, 1977; and R. Simon, *Gramsci's Political Thought*, 1982. On religion see H. McLeod, *Religion and the Working Class in Nineteenth-Century Britain*, 1984, and on education see M. Sanderson, *Education, Economic Change and Society in England 1780–1870*, 1983, and their excellent bibliographies.

44 J. Stevenson, *Popular Disturbances in England 1700–1870*, 1979 is a convenient introduction with a full bibliography and can usefully be supplemented with the broader approach of G. Rude, *Ideology and Popular Protest*, 1980. On the legitimating role of custom see B. Bushaway, *By Rite*, 1982; and J. M. Golby and A. W. Purdue, *The Civilization of the Crowd*, 1984

45 E. P. Thompson, 'The Moral Economy of the English Crowd in the Eighteenth Century', *Past and Present*, no. 50, 1971, p. 79

46 A great deal has been written on this recently but see J. Stevenson, *Popular Disturbances in England 1700–1870*, 1979; and A. Charlesworth (ed.), *An Atlas of Rural Protest in Britain 1548–1900*, 1983, pp. 63–118

47 M. I. Thomis, *The Luddites*, 1970, gives one interpretation and E. P. Thompson, *The Making of the English Working Class*, 1963, another

48 On this see A. Charlesworth (ed.), *An Atlas of Rural Protest in Britain 1548–1900*, 1983; J. P. D. Dunbabin, *Rural Discontent in Nineteenth Century Britain*, 1974, especially pp. 11–61; on Wales, D. Jones, *Before Rebecca*, 1973; on Ireland, G. Rude, *Protest and Punishment*, OUP, 1978; on Scotland, E. Richards, *A History of Highland Clearances*, vol. 1, Croom Helm, 1982

49 The standard work is E. J. Hobsbawm and G. Rude, *Captain Swing*, 1973

50 The most accessible books on social and political reform up to the 1850s are D. Frazer, *The Evolution of the British Welfare State*, 2nd edn, 1984; U. R. Q. Henriques, *Before the Welfare State*, Longman, 1979; O. MacDonagh, *Early Victorian Government*, 1977; and J. Roach, *Social Reform in England 1780–1880*, 1979

51 A. J. P. Taylor, *Laissez-faire and State Intervention in Nineteenth-Century Britain*, 1972 summarises the debate.

52 A. Brundage, *The Making of the New Poor Law*, 1978

53 *Ibid.*, p. 182

54 *Ibid.*, p. 183

55 D. Fraser, *Urban Politics in Victorian England*, Leicester University Press, 1976, pp. 55–90

56 N. Gash, *Politics in the Age of Peel*, 2nd edn, 1978
57 D. C. Moore, *The Politics of Deference*, 1976 and M. Brock, *The Great Reform Act*, 1973, pp. 314–36
58 P. Joyce, *Work, Society and Politics – the culture of the factory in later Victorian England*, 1980, gives an excellent discussion of this issue, especially pp. 90–157. On the persistence of deferential values see H. Newby, *The Deferential Worker*, 1978
59 *Ibid.*, p. 93

1 The agricultural experience – society and conditions

Between 1800 and 1850 the focal point of both economic activity and population growth moved irrevocably from rural to urban settings. The reasons for this lie in the changing nature of farming as well as in the dynamism of the industrial sectors. In 1800 Robert Bloomfield wrote in 'The Farmer's Boy' that,

> Whene'er refinement shows its hated face:
> . . . 'tis the Peasant's curse:
> That hourly makes his wretched station worse.

The key word here is 'refinement'. On the one hand it could apply to those 'refinements' in organisation and technique which historians have called the Agricultural Revolution. But it could also have a social meaning, especially when related to the idea of 'his wretched station'. It is the aim of this chapter to look at these economic and social changes in rural society. Was there a lowering of the living standards of the agricultural labourer in the period 1800–50?

Look at these two contrasting views of the impact of enclosure.

1.1 John Clare on enclosure

> Far spread the moory ground, a level scene
> Bespread with rush and one eternal green,
> That never felt the rage of blundering plough,
> Though centuries wreathed spring blossoms on its brow.
> Autumn met plains that stretched them far away
> In unchecked shadows of green, brown and grey.
> Unbounded freedom ruled the wandering scene;
> No fence of ownership crept in between
> To hide the prospect from the gazing eye . . .
> Enclosure came, and trampled on the grave

Of labour's rights, and left the poor a slave;
And memory's pride, ere want to wealth did bow,
Is both the shadow and the substance now.
The sheep and cows were free to range as then
Where change might prompt, nor felt the bonds of men.   15
Cows went and came with every morn and night
To the wild pasture as their common right . . .
Fence meeting fence in owner's little bounds
Of field and meadow, large as garden-grounds,
In little parcels little minds to please,   20
With men and flocks imprisoned, ill at ease . . .

'Enclosure' by John Clare, printed in J. Reeves (ed.), *Selected Poems
of John Clare*, Heinemann 1954, pp. 22–3

1.2   An alternative view

Inclose, inclose, ye swains!
Why will you joy in common field, where pitch,
Noxious to wool must stain your motley flock
To mark your property? . . . Besides, in fields
Promiscuous held all culture languishes;   5
The glebe, exhausted, thin supplies received;
Dull waters rest upon the rushy flats
And barren furrows; none the rising grove
There plants for late posterity, nor hedge
To shield the flock, nor copse for cheering fire;   10
And in the distant village every hearth
Devours the grassy sward, the verdant food
Of injur'd herds and flocks, or what the plough
Should turn and moulder for the bearded grain . . .
Add too, the idle pilf'rer easier there   15
Eludes detection, when the lamb or ewe
From intermingled flocks he steals; or when,
With loosen'd tether of his horse or cow,
The milky stalk of the tall green-ear'd corn,
The year's slow rip'ning fruit, the anxious hope   20
Of his laborious neighbour, he destroys.

From 'The Carmarthenshire Painter–Poet', John Dyer, printed in
G. E. Mingay, *Rural Life in Victorian England*, Heinemann, 1977, p. 16

Questions

1   How does John Clare describe the open-field system [1.1]?
2   In what ways is Clare's view of the nature of agriculture before and after enclosure a 'romantic' one?
3   What material benefits and farming improvements does John Dyer identify as resulting from the enclosure of land [1.2]? How do they conflict with Clare's conclusions.
4   How was land ownership affected by enclosure between 1780 and 1830?
5   Liberation or bondage? Discuss these two views which dominated contemporary attitudes to enclosure.

The *Annals of Agriculture* and the various county 'General Views' are crucial sources on the economic and social effects of enclosure.

1.3   Arthur Young in 1801

The fact is, that by nineteen enclosure bills in twenty the Poor are injured, in some grossly injured. It may be said that the commissioners are sworn to do justice. What is that to the people who suffer? It must be generally known that they suffer in their own opinions, and yet enclosures go on by commissioners, who take away   5
the poor people's cows wherever they come, as well as those kept legally as those which are not. What is it to the poor man to be told that the Houses of Parliament are extremely tender of property, while the father of the family is forced to sell his cow and his land because the one is not competent to the other; and being deprived of the only   10
motive for industry, squanders the money, contracts bad habits, enlists for a soldier, and leaves the wife and children to the parish? If enclosures were beneficial to the poor, rates would not rise as in other parishes after an act to enclose. The poor in these parishes may say, and with truth, 'Parliament may be tender of property; all I know is,   15
I had a cow, and an act of Parliament has taken it from me.'

A. Young, *An Inquiry in to the Propriety of applying Wastes, etc.,*
1801

1.4   Arthur Young in 1804

The common was very extensive. I conversed with a farmer and several cottagers, one of them said enclosing would ruin England; it

would be worse than ten years ago. I asked him what he had already lost from enclosure. He replied that he had kept four cows before the parish had been enclosed, and now he did not keep so much as a   5
goose. All declared that they could see no advantage in enclosure.

A. Young, printed in the *Annals of Agriculture*, vol. xlii, 1804

1.5   W. Pitt in 1807

The Duke is a kind landlord, never oppresses and seldom removes a tenant. The advanced rent has been in part produced by the enclosure, but in part certainly by the change of time and circumstances; the land has been much improved by laying the richest part to grass and by drainage etc.; the occupations are mostly   5
small, few individuals rent above £100 in an estate of £21,000 per annum. A numerous and able bodied peasantry is now supported; – poor rates low, rents well paid –. The enclosure of this Vale has not at all, I believe, hitherto lessened the number of its inhabitants, as the farms are small and few changes in tenantry have taken place.   10

W. Pitt, *A General View of Leicestershire*, 1807

Questions

1   Explain the difference between the attitudes of Young and Pitt to the impact of enclosure.
2   What does Young mean by 'the Houses of Parliament are extremely tender of property' [1.3, line 8]?
3   What are the consequences of enclosure that Young identifies? Is he over-pessimistic in his analysis?
4   The effects of enclosure varied in different parts of Britain. Why?
5   Enclosure was concerned with legal rights rather than justice. Discuss.
6   Propaganda for and against enclosure makes accurate historical judgement difficult. How true is this statement?

Between 1793 and 1815 Britain was almost continually at war. Farmers and landowners enjoyed great prosperity and the edges of cultivation were pushed back. Land which was totally unsuitable for arable farming, like some of the chalk lands, was brought into use. Large profits and rising rents made this possible. But this trend was reversed after 1813 and from then to the 1840s British farming went through a difficult period. Enclosure continued, though in highland Scotland it was from arable to pasture. Wheat farmers faced severe problems. Prices fell – wheat was 127 shillings a quarter in 1812, but had collapsed to 74 shillings a quarter within two years. Farmers sought protection from parliament – the controversial Corn Law of 1815 was the result. Wages were cut. Labour was reduced – a process speeded up by the mechanisation of farming after 1830, though not widespread before 1850. Farming Associations proliferated throughout the country. The economic role of farmers was clearly stated.

1.6 Farmers holding the 'principal pass' of England's economic system

In half an hour's walk from every market place in the kingdom you find yourself under the sway of these powerful and responsible, though unassuming potentates. Once among green fields and hedgerows, and the tenant-farmer is your immediate superior. The road you are riding on is his, the ditch you leap over, and the bridge   5
you cross are maintained by him. If you damage a fence it is his. The cattle are his. The labourers are in his pay, and the cottages are in his letting. He keeps the carpenter's bench, the sawpit and the forge incessantly at work. The village shop and the village public house are filled by his servants and his labourers. If profits fall, he has to draw   10
on his capital to keep things going. If wages are reduced, he has to bear the odium. If disaffection spread, his ricks are burnt. When he can no longer pay wages, he must still pay rates.

An anonymous leader from *The Times*, 23 December 1850

1.7 The rapacity of landlords

Safe in their barns, these Sabine tillers sent
Their bretheren out to battle – why? for rent!
Year after Year they voted cent per cent,
Blood, sweat and tear-wrung millions, – why? for rent!
They roar'd, they dined, they drank, they swore they meant   5
To die for England – why then live? – for rent!
The peace has made one general malcontent
Of these high-market patriots; war was rent!
Their love of country, millions all misspent,
How reconcile? by reconciling rent!   10
And will they no repay the treasures lent?

No: down with everything, and up with rent!
Their good, ill, health, wealth, joy or discontent,
Being, end, aim, religion – rent, rent, rent!

Lord Byron, 'The Age of Bronze', 1816

Questions

1   How does *The Times* succeed in bringing out the idea of tenant-farmers having both rights and responsibilities in 1850 [1.6]?
2   How accurate is Lord Byron's analysis of the impact of war and peace upon British agriculture [1.7]?
3   In what ways had agriculture changed between 1816 and 1850? Are these enough to explain the differences between documents 1.6 and 1.7?
4   'Depression' is a term historians need to use carefully with reference to British farming between 1815 and the mid 1830s. Discuss.
5   Between 1800 and 1850 the possession and farming of land ceased to be of major importance. The repeal of the Corn Laws in 1846 ended the monopoly of the landed interest. Evaluate these statements.

Falling prices should have meant relative prosperity for labourers, assuming that they were in regular employment at a steady rate of pay. But farmers reduced both wages and labour to protect themselves.

1.8   William Cobbett

All of you who are 60 years of age can recollect that bread and meat and not wretched potatoes were the food of the labouring people; you can recollect that every industrious labouring man brewed his own beer and drank it by his own fireside . . . you can recollect when the young people were able to provide money before they were married   5
to purchase decent furniture for a house, and had no need to go to the parish to furnish them with a miserable nest to creep into; you can recollect when a bastard child was a rarity in a village . . . when every sober and industrious labourer had his Sunday coat . . . when a young man was pointed at if he had not on a Sunday a decent coat   10
upon his back, a good hat upon his head, a clean shirt with silk handkerchief round his neck, leather breeches without a spot, whole worsted stockings tied under the knee with a red garter, a pair of handsome Sunday shoes . . . [with] silver buckles.

William Cobbett, *Twopenny Trash*, 1831

1.9

Thirty-five years ago the Agricultural Labourer possessed a home to
shelter him, a family to comfort him and food to sustain him. In
most cases he was either a resident on the farm where he laboured, or
lived in a cottage in a neighbouring village. Where he was without
the reach of coal, he gathered wood, furze or turf with little or no   5
molestation . . . his garden was indeed small and ill cultivated. The
value of potatoes was neither so well known or so highly appreciated
as it is at present; and the idea of subsiding upon potatoes alone, as
an article of food, was not entertained by the labourer of England.
Bread was made at home, which, though coarser than that in present   10
use, was not on that account less nourishing food for the labouring
man. In times of distress bread and water sustained him at his last
extremity.

Thomas Postans, A Letter to Sir Thomas Baring, Bt., MP, 1831

1.10   Weekly budget of Robert Crick, 1842

		Family earnings		Family expenditure*
Robert Crick	(42)	9s 0d	Bread	9s 0d
Wife	(40)	9d	Potatoes	1s 0d
Boy	(12)	2s 0d	Rent	1s 2d
Boy	(11)	1s 0d	Tea	2d
Boy	(8)	1s 0d	Sugar	2d
Girl	(6)	—	Soap	3d
Girl	(4)	—	Blue	$\frac{1}{2}d$
			Thread etc.	2d
			Candles	3d
			Salt	$\frac{1}{2}d$
			Coal/wood	$9\frac{1}{2}d$
			Butter	$4\frac{1}{2}d$
			Cheese	3d
Total		13s 9d		13s 9d

* Amounts in shillings (s) and pence (d); 12d = 1s (5p); 20s = £1 (100p)

**Weekly budget of Robert Crick, farm labourer from Lavenham,
Suffolk, based on *Report on the Employment of Women and
Children in Agriculture*, Parliamentary Papers XII, 1843, p. 233**

1.11   Low wages and over-supply of labour

The wages of labour are lower on Salisbury Plain than in
Dorsetshire, and lower than in the dairy and arable districts of North
Wilts. An explanation of this may partly be found in the fact, that the
command of wages is altogether under the control of the large
farmers, some of whom employ the whole labour of the parish. Six   5
shillings a week was the amount given for ordinary labourers by the
most extensive farmer in South Wilts . . . 7s however, is the more
common rate and out of that the labourer has to pay 1s a week for
the rent of his cottage. If prices continue low, it is said that even
these wages must be reduced . . . Both farmers and labourers suffer   10
in this locality from the present over-supply of labour. The farmer is
compelled to employ more men than his present mode of operations
require, and, to save himself, he pays them a lower rate of wages than
is sufficient to give that amount of physical power which is necessary
for the performance of a fair day's work. His labour is, therefore,   15
really more costly than where sufficient wages are paid.

James Caird, *English Agriculture in 1850–1*, 1852

1.12   High and low wage areas

The last class of the agricultural body whose interests we have to
consider, is the labourer. The disparity of wages paid for the same
nominal amount of work in the various counties of England is so
great as to show that there must be something in the present state of
the law affecting the labourer which prevents the wages of the   5
agricultural labourer finding a more natural level throughout the
country. Taking the highest rate we have met with – 15s per week in
parts of Lancashire, and comparing it with the lowest – 6s in south
Wilts . . . We again divide the country into the two divisions of the
corn counties of the east and south coast; and the mixed corn and   10
grass of the midlands and western counties . . . The black line,
dotted on the map, indicates the limit southwards of the coal
formation . . . the higher wages of the northern counties is altogether
due to the proximity of manufacturing and mining enterprise . . .
The influence of manufacturing enterprise is thus seen to add 37 per 15
cent to the wages of the northern counties as compared with those of
the south. The line is distinctly drawn at the point where coal ceases

OUTLINE MAP OF ENGLAND,

Shewing the distinction between the Corn and Grazing counties; and the line of division between high and low Wages.

All to the East of the black line, running from North to South, may be regarded as the chief Corn Districts of England; the average rental per acre of the cultivated land of which is 30 per cent. less than that of the counties to the West of the same line, which are the principal Grazing, Green Crop, and Dairy districts.

The dotted line, running from East to West, shows the line of Wages; the average of the counties to the North of that line being 37 per cent. higher than those to the South of it.

to be found, to the south of which there is only one of the counties we visited in which the wages reach 10s a week, Sussex. The local circumstances of that county explain the cause of labour being there   20 better remunerated; the wealthy population of Brighton, and other places on the Sussex coast, affording an increased market for labour beyond the demands of agriculture.

James Caird, *English Agriculture in 1850–51*, 1852

Questions

1   In what ways do documents **1.8** and **1.9** exaggerate the prosperity of labourers in the late eighteenth century? In what ways does propaganda like this influence historians in their analysis of changes in farming?

2   The standard of living of agricultural labourers deteriorated in the first half of the nineteenth century. Discuss this proposition with reference to documents **1.8**, **1.9** and **1.10**.

3   Why, according to James Caird [**1.11 and 1.12**] were wages low in southern England?

4   How does Caird explain the variation in wages in southern England in document **1.11**?

5   Agricultural wages were lower in southern England because of an over-supply of labour. Discuss.

6   Alternative sources of employment pushed up wages in farming. How does document **1.12** demonstrate this?

7   Why should historians look beyond wage rates when considering whether the standard of living of farm workers fell in the first half of the nineteenth century?

8   Machines played little part in declining living standards in farming areas. How true is this statement?

The final part of this chapter is a case study of Little Wratting, a village community in Suffolk, based on the 1851 Census returns.

1.13(a) Population in Little Wratting 1801–91

1801	107	1851	212
1811	141	1861	193
1821	183	1871	217
1831	212	1881	267
1841	239	1891	220

Census returns, 1891

1.13(b) Gazetteer

WRATTING (LITTLE) is a small village in a pleasant valley, 2 miles NE of Haverhill, and adjoining Great Wratting in the south. It has in its parish 239 souls and 950 acres of fertile land, all freehold and belonging to Mrs Lucy Bird, Mrs Frost, Wm Margetts, Esq., Mrs C. Jardine and a few small proprietors. The Church is a small   5 ancient structure, and the benefice is a rectory, valued in K.B. [King's Book] at £4 19s 9d . . . The principal inhabitants are Edwin Binks, shopkeeper; John Goodchild, farmer, Wash; Mrs Caroline Jardine; Wm Owers, Hill farm; and Charles Punchard, corn miller and farmer, Blunts Hall.

William White, *History, Gazetteer and Directory of Suffolk*, 1844, p. 749

1.13(c) Census Enumerators' Returns 1851

Little Wratting 1851

49

No.	Add.	Name	Relation to Head of Fam.	M/U	Age M	Age F	Rank/Prof/Occup.	Where born
1.	Wash Farm	Thomas Frost	Head	M	34		Farmer, 210 acres emp. 11 labs. 3 carpenters	Suffolk, Cowlinge.
	*Do.	Mary Frost	Wife	M		26	Farmer's Wife	Do. Haverhill.
	Do.	Hannah Goodchild	Serv.	U		17	House Servant	Do. Thurlow.
2.	Blunts Hall	Chas Punchard	Head	M	43		Farmer, 500 acres emp. 30 labs.	Do. Pakenham.
	Do.	Elizabeth Do.	Wife	M		44	Farmer's Wife	Do. Haverhill.
	Do.	Ellen Do.	Dau			16	Farmer's Daughter	Do. Lt. Wratting.
	Do.	Frank Do.	Son		8		Farmer's Son	Do. Do.
	Do.	Elizabeth Do.	Dau			5	Farmer's Daughter	Do. Do.
	Do.	Deborah Binks	Serv.	U		18	House Servant	Do. Do.
	Do.	Frances Hazelwood	Serv.	U		18	House Servant	Do. Bardwell.
3.	Haverhill Rd.	Thomas Cornell	Head	M	41		Farm Labourer	Do. Lt. Wratting.
	Do.	Sarah Do.	Wife	M		34		Do. Do.
	Do.	Mary Binks	Niece	U		11		Do. Do.
4.	Haverhill Rd.	John Martin	Head	M	62		Farm Labourer & Shepherd	Essex, Sturmer.
	Do.	Letitia Do.	Wife	M		62		Suffolk, Hundon.
	Do.	John Do.	Grandson	U	12			Do. Do.
	Do.	Henry Smith	Lodger	U	18			Do. Lt. Wratting.
5.	Haverhill Rd.	William Lamprill	Head	M	36			Do. Do.
	Do.	Harriet Do.	Wife	M		34		Do. Do.
	Do.	George Do.	Son	U	11			Do. Do.
6.	Haverhill Rd.	Isaac Brown	Head	M	74		Farm Labourer	Do. Kedington.

No.	Add.	Name	Relation to Head of Fam.	M/U	Age M	Age F	Rank/Prof/Occup.	Where born	
	Do.	Mary Do.	Wife	M		76		Do.	Do.
	Do.	John Do.	Son	U	41		Farm Labourer	Do.	Lt. Wratting.
	Do.	James Do.	Son	Widr	36		Farm Labourer	Do.	Do.
7.	Haverhill Rd.	Samuel Bailey	Head	M	38		Farm Labourer	Suffolk,	Lt. Wratting
	Do.	Susan Do.	Wife	M		42		Do.	Do.
	Do.	Eliza Do.	Dau	U		13		Do.	Do.
	Do.	Henry Do.	Son		11		Do.	Do.	Do.
	Do.	Samuel Do.	Son		9			Do.	Do.
	Do.	Susannah Do.	Dau			7		Do.	Do.
	Do.	William Do.	Son		5		Do.	Do.	Do.
	Do.	Joseph Do.	Son		11		Do.	Do.	Do.
8.	Haverhill Rd.	Chas Humphrey	Head	M	50		Farm Labourer	Kedington.	Do.
	Do.	Mary Do.	Wife	M		46		Lt. Wratting.	Do.
	Do.	George Do.	Son	U	20		Farm Labourer	Do.	Do.
	Do.	Frances Do.	Dau			11		Do.	Do.
	Do.	Caroline Do.	Dau			7		Do.	Do.
	Do.	Eliza Do.	Dau					Do.	Do.
	Do.	Joseph Binks	Lodger		20		Farm Labourer	Do.	Do.
9.	Wilsey Farm	Simon Garrad	Head	M	35		Farm Bailiff, 120 acres 13 labs.	Suffolk,	Ashfield.
	Do.	Elizabeth Do.	Wife	M		23		Do.	Kedington.
	Do.	Simon Do.	Son		4mths			Do.	Lt. Wratting.
10.	Wilsey Farm	Henry Brown	Head	M	30		Farm Labourer	Do.	Kedington.
	Do.	Mary Ann Do.	Wife	M		24		Do.	Haverhill.
	Do.	Henry Pask	Lodger	U	46		Farm Labourer	Do.	Kedington.
11.	Chapel Farm	John Diggens	Head	M	66		Farmer, 163 acres 18 labs.	Do.	Walsham-le-Willows.
	Do.	Mary Ann Do.	Wife	M		63		Do.	Buxhall.

No.	Address	Name	Relation	Condition	Age	Occupation	County	Place of Birth
	Do.	Edmund Do.	Son	U	42	Farmer's Son	Do.	Walsham-le-Willows.
	Do.	Samuel Do.	Son	U	22	Farmer's Son	Do.	Gt. Wratting.
	Do.	Frederick Do.	Son	U	20	Farmer's Son	Do.	Do.
	Do.	James Scotcher	Grandson	U	11		Do.	Haverhill.
	Do.	James Malton	Serv.		15		Do.	Do.
12.	Haverhill Rd.	Benjamin Buffels	Head	M	66	Farm Labourer	Do.	Gt. Wratting.
	Do.	Rebecca Do.	Wife	M	66		Do.	Withersfield.
13.	Haverhill Rd.	Charles Coote	Head	M	40	Farm Labourer	Essex,	Steeple Bumpstead.
	Do.	Rebecca Do.	Wife	M	43		Essex,	Stoke
	Do.	Eliza Do.	Dau	U	22		Suffolk,	Lt. Wratting.
	Do.	Ann Do.	Dau	U	11		Do.	Do.
	Do.	Joseph Do.	Son	U	6		Do.	Do.
	Do.	William Preston	Son-in-law	U	9		Do.	Do.
	Do.	George Preston	Do. Do.	U	2		Do.	Do.
14.	Haverhill Rd.	Abraham Smoothy	Head	M	38	Farm Labourer	Suffolk,	Lt. Wratting.
	Do.	Sophia Do.	Wife	M	39		Do.	Hundon.
	Do.	William Do.	Son	U	16		Do.	Lt. Wratting
	Do.	Ann Do.	Dau		9		Do.	Lt. Wratting.
15.	Haverhill Rd.	John Lovedy	Head	M	35	Farm Labourer	Do.	Lt. Wratting.
	Do.	Margaret Do.	Wife	M	32		Do.	Kedington.
	Do.	Harriet Bowyer	Dau-in-law	U	11		Do.	Kedington.
16.	Haverhill Rd.	James Cornell	Head	M	29	Farm Labourer	Do.	Lt. Wratting.
	Do.	Caroline Do.	Wife	M	29		Cambs.	
	Do.	William Do.	Son	U	2		Suffolk,	Lt. Wratting.
17.	Haverhill Rd.	Joseph Binks	Head	Wid	38	Farm Labourer	Suffolk,	Lt. Wratting.
	Do.	Harriet Do.	Dau	U	15		Do.	Do.
	Do.	Eliza Do.	Dau	U	13		Do.	Do.
	Do.	Elija Do.	Son	U	10		Do.	Do.
18.	Haverhill Rd.	George Baker	Head	M	39	Farm Labourer	Do.	Do.

No.	Add.	Name		Relation to Head of Fam.	M/U	Age M	Age F	Rank/Prof/Occup.	Where born	
	Do.	Madeline	Do.	Wife	M		40		Do.	Haverhill.
	Do.	George	Do.	Son	U	18			Do.	Haverhill.
	Do.	Mary Ann	Do.	Dau	U		16		Do.	Lt. Wratting.
	Do.	John	Do.	Son	U	13			Do.	Haverhill.
	Do.	William	Do.	Son	U	9			Do.	Haverhill.
19.	Haverhill Rd.	John Turner	Do.	Head	M	25		Farm Labourer	Suffolk,	Lt. Wratting.
	Do.	Emma	Do.	Wife	M		24		Do.	Do.
	Do.	Thomas	Do.	Son	U	6			Do.	Do.
	Do.	Rachael	Do.	Dau			4		Do.	Do.
	Do.	James	Do.	Son	U	1			Do.	Do.
20.	Haverhill Rd.	Lydia Lovedy	Do.	Head	Wid		40		Do.	Do.
	Do.	Adelaide	Do.	Dau	Wid		19		Do.	Do.
	Do.	Anna	Do.	Dau	U		15		Do.	Do.
	Do.	Ellen	Do.	Dau	U		10		Do.	Do.
	Do.	Harriet	Do.	Dau	U		5		Do.	Do.
	Do.	Angelina	Do.	Dau	U		2		Do.	Do.
21.	Haverhill Rd.	James Lovedy	Do.	Head	U	40			Do.	Do.
	Do.	Anne	Do.	Sister	U		27		Do.	Do.
22.	Haverhill Rd.	Sarah Cornell	Do.	Head	Wid		68		Suffolk,	Kedington.
	Do.	William	Do.	Son	U	32			Do.	Lt. Wratting.
	Do.	Anne	Do.	Dau	U		38		Do.	Do.
	Do.	Deborah	Do.	Grand-dau	U		11		Do.	Do.
	Do.	Thomas	Do.	Grandson	U	2			Do.	Do.
23.	Haverhill Rd.	John Smith	Do.	Head	M	41		Farm Labourer	Do.	Baythorn End.
	Do.	Alice	Do.	Wife	M		35		Do.	Barton Mills.
	Do.	Elizabeth	Do.	Dau	U		12		Do.	Lt. Wratting.
	Do.	Harriet	Do.	Dau	U		11		Do.	Do.
	Do.	Robert	Do.	Son		9			Do.	Do.

No.	Address	Name	Relation	Cond.	Age (M)	Age (F)	Occupation	County	Parish
	Do.	Eliza Do.	Dau			6		Do.	Do.
24.	Haverhill Rd.	George Martin	Head	M	41		Farm Labourer	Do.	Do.
	Do.	Charlotte Do.	Wife	M		42		Do.	Do.
	Do.	Joseph Do.	Son	U	19		Labourer's Son	Do.	Do.
	Do.	Mary Ann Do.	Dau	U		17	Labourer's Dau	Do.	Do.
	Do.	William Do.	Son	U	15			Do.	Do.
	Do.	David Do.	Son	U	13			Do.	Do.
	Do.	Maria Do.	Dau	U		11		Do.	Do.
	Do.	George Do.	Son		9			Do.	Do.
	Do.	Elijah Do.	Son		7			Do.	Do.
	Do.	Henry Do.	Son		5			Do.	Do.
25.	Haverhill Rd.	Jonathan Martin	Head	M	59		Farm Labourer	Do.	Do.
	Do.	Jane Do.	Wife	M		50		Do.	Freckenham.
26.	Haverhill Rd.	Stephen Free	Head	M	35		Farm Labourer	Suffolk,	Lt. Wratting.
	Do.	Charlotte Do.	Wife	M		30		Do.	Wickhambrook.
	Do.	William Do.	Son		9			Do.	Lt. Wratting.
	Do.	Mary Ann Do.	Dau			6		Do.	Do.
	Do.	Sophia Do.	Dau			4		Do.	Do.
	Do.	John Do.	Son		2			Do.	Do.
	Do.	Edward Cook	Nephew		7			Do.	Wickhambrook.
27.	Haverhill Rd.	Joseph Lovedy	Head	M	55		Farm Labourer	Do.	Lt. Wratting.
	Do.	Sarah Do.	Wife	M		50		Essex,	Steeple Bumpstead.
	Do.	Caroline Do.	Dau	U		24		Suffolk,	Lt. Wratting.
	Do.	Eliza Do.	Dau	U		21		Do.	Do.
	Do.	Matilda Do.	Dau	U		20		Do.	Do.
	Do.	James Do.	Son	U	19		Farm Labourer	Do.	Do.
	Do.	Harriet Do.	Dau	U		15		Do.	Do.
	Do.	Joseph Do.	Son	U	14			Do.	Do.
	Do.	William Do.	Son	U	11			Do.	Do.
	Do.	Elijah Do.	Son		8			Do.	Do.
	Do.	Frederick Do.	Son		5			Do.	Do.
	Do.	Frank Do.	Son		4			Do.	Do.

No.	Add.	Name	Relation to Head of Fam.	M/U	Age M	Age F	Rank/Prof/Occup.	Where born
28.	Haverhill Rd.	James Binks	Head	M	44			Do.
	Do.	Martha Do.	Wife	M		44		Kedington.
	Do.	Mary Ann Do.	Dau	U		16		Lt. Wratting.
	Do.	William Do.	Son	U	13			Do.
	Do.	Mary Do.	Dau			3		Do.
29.	Haverhill Rd.	William Barber	Head	M	52		Farm Labourer	Suffolk,
	Do.	Ellen Do.	Wife	M		49		Kedington.
	Do.	David Do.	Son	U	20			Do.
	Do.	Hannah Do.	Dau	U		16		Lt. Wratting.
	Do.	Ellen Do.	Dau	U		14		Do.
	Do.	Charles Do.	Son		12			Do.
	Do.	John Do.	Son		10			Do.
	Do.	William Do.	Son		6			Do.
30.	Haverhill Rd.	Thomas Smith	Head	M	59		Farm Labourer	Gt. Wratting.
	Do.	Mary Do.	Wife	M		57		Kedington.
	Do.	Ann Do.	Dau	U		20		Lt. Wratting.
31.	Haverhill Rd.	James Hicks	Head	M	54		Farm Bailiff. 80 acres emp. 6 labs.	Creating.
	Do.	Mary Do.	Wife	M		64		Watson.
32.	Haverhill Rd.	John Binks	Head	M	47		Farm Labourer	Lt. Wratting.
	Do.	Mary Do.	Wife	M		44		Haverhill.
	Do.	Emily Do.	Dau	U		13		Lt. Wratting.
	Do.	Ellen Do.	Dau	U		10		Do.
	Do.	Susannah Binks	Dau	U		6		Do.
	Do.	Elizabeth Do.	Dau	U		4		Do.
	Do.	William Do.	Son		4			Do.
33.	Haverhill Rd.	James Turner	Head	M	40		Farm Labourer	Do.
	Do.	Harriet Do.	Wife	M		36		Gt. Wratting.

No.	Address	Name		Relation	Condition	Age	Occupation	County	Parish
	Do.	Sarah	Do.	Mother	Wid	77		Do.	Haverhill.
34.	Haverhill Rd.	Mary Turner	Do.	Head	Wid	37		Suffolk.	Lt. Wratting.
	Do.	Charles	Do.	Son	U	15		Do.	Do.
	Do.	Mary	Do.	Dau	U	13		Do.	Do.
	Do.	Robert	Do.	Son		7		Do.	Do.
	Do.	Rebecca	Do.	Dau		3		Do.	Do.
35.	Haverhill Rd.	Thomas Smith	Do.	Head	M	25	Farm Labourer	Do.	Do.
	Do.	Mary	Do.	Wife	M	23		Essex,	Helions Bumpstead.
	Do.	William	Do.	Son		2		Suffolk,	Lt. Wratting.
36.	Haverhill Rd.	Anne Turner	Do.	Head	Wid	49		Do.	Kedington.
	Do.	David	Do.	Son	U	17	Farm Labourer	Do.	Lt. Wratting.
	Do.	Elijah	Do.	Son	U	15	Farm Labourer	Do.	Do.
	Do.	Eliza	Do.	Dau	U	13		Do.	Do.
	Do.	Hester	Do.	Dau	U	11		Do.	Do.
	Do.	Thomasine	Do.	Dau	U	9		Do.	Do.
	Do.	James	Do.	Son		6		Do.	Do.
	Do.	Thomas	Do.	Son		4		Do.	Do.
37.	Haverhill Rd.	George Turner	Do.	Head	M	26	Farm Labourer	Do.	Do.
	Do.	Elizabeth	Do.	Wife	M	26		Do.	Do.
	Do.	Elijah	Do.	Son		6		Do.	Do.
	Do.	Alfred	Do.	Son		4		Do.	Do.
	Do.	Henry	Do.	Son		2		Do.	Do.
38.	Ardwick Arms	Isaac Brown	Do.	Head	M	38	Coal Carter	Suffolk,	Lt. Wratting.
	Do.	Sarah	Do.	Wife	M	34		Do.	Do.
	Do.	Elizabeth	Do.	Dau		9		Do.	Do.
	Do.	Ann	Do.	Dau		7		Do.	Do.
	Do.	Ellen	Do.	Dau		5		Do.	Do.
	Do.	Hester	Do.	Dau		4		Do.	Do.
	Do.	Stephen	Do.	Son		2		Do.	Do.
	Do.	Harriet	Do.	Dau		1 mth		Do.	Do.

No.	Add.	Name	Relation to Head of Fam.	M/U	Age M	Age F	Rank/Prof/Occup.	Where born	
	Do.	Thomas West	Serv.	U	18		Farm Labourer	Do.	Haverhill.
	Do.	William Rowlinson	Lodger	U	29		Farm Labourer	Do.	Gt. Wratting.
39.	Kedington Rd.	Edwin Binks	Head	M	55		Baker	Do.	Lt. Wratting.
	Do.	Elizabeth Do.	Wife	M		62		Essex,	Helions Bumpstead.
	Do.	Frances Do.	Dau	U		15		Suffolk,	Lt. Wratting
	Do.	Nathan Preston	Lodger	U	15			Do.	Do.
40.	Kedington Rd.	George Free	Head	M	50		Farm Labourer	Do.	Do.
	Do.	Elizabeth Free	Wife	M		50		Essex,	Sturmer.
	Do.	William Do.	Son	U	28		Farm Labourer	Suffolk,	Lt. Wratting.
	Do.	Thomas Do.	Son	U	19		Farm Labourer	Do.	Do.
	Do.	Harriet Do.	Dau			10		Do.	Do.
	Do.	Elizabeth Do.	Dau			5		Do.	Do.
	Do.	Mary Ann Do.	Dau			3		Do.	Do.
41.	Kedington Rd.	John Smoothy	Head	M	63		Farm Labourer	Essex,	Wixoe.
	Do.	Margaret Do.	Wife	M		58		Suffolk,	Hundon.
42.	Haverhill Rd.	William Taylor	Head	Widr	67		Farm Labourer	Do.	Lt. Wratting.
	Do.	William Do.	Son	U	26		Farm Labourer	Do.	Gt. Wratting.
	Do.	David Do.	Son	U	23		Farm Labourer	Do.	Do.
	Do.	Eliza French	Niece	U		21	Servant	Do.	Barnardiston.

One house uninhabited

*Do. = ditto

Questions

A   Find your way round the Census: population structure

1   In 1851, how many of the following were there in Little Wratting?
  (i)   men
  (ii) women
  (iii) married men, unmarried men and widowers aged 16 or over
  (iv) males under 16
  (v)   married women, unmarried women and widows aged 16 or over
  (vi) females under 16
2   How many men and women were there between the ages of 0–5, 6–10, 11–15, 16–20 and so on up to 66–70 and over 70? Show this information in the form of a pyramid graph. What conclusions can you draw from this about the age distribution in Little Wratting?
3   How many children were there in each household? What was the average size of family? It is possible to identify any difference between the family size of agricultural labourers and other occupational groups?
4   Draw together your information on population in Little Wratting and write a brief explanatory account of your statistics (maximum 300 words).

B   Find your way round the census: occupations and birthplaces

1   Make a list of the stated 'rank/prof/occup' for Little Wratting. How many people fall into each category?
2   What information can you 'squeeze' from the Census about the following in Little Wratting?
  (i)   farmers
  (ii) agricultural labourers
  (iii) farm bailiffs
  (iv) land tenure

3   On 23 October 1850, the following advertisement appeared in the
Bury and Norwich Post:

THEATRE ROYAL, BURY,

Under the Sole Management of Mr. HOOPER,
Late Manager of the St. James's Theatre, London, and
Manager of the Theatre Royal, Bath and Brighton,
who has become Lessee of this Theatre for a term of
years.

On WEDNESDAY next, Nov. 6th, under the Patronage of
J. JOSSELYN. ESQ.,
AND THE
Gentlemen of the Suffolk Hunt,
The Comedy of
USED UP,
AFTER WHICH,
Faint Heart never Won Fair Lady;
To conclude with
BOX AND COX.

*The Performance each evening to commence at Seven, and
terminate before Eleven o'clock.*
The Box Office open daily from Eleven to Three o'clock,
under the direction of Mr. Lancaster.

The entire population of Little Wratting has, among others, been
invited to attend. Place them on the seating plan of the present
Theatre Royal at Bury St Edmunds. The most expensive seats are in
the dress circle and the grand circle boxes. The grand circle is less
expensive and the stalls are the cheapest.

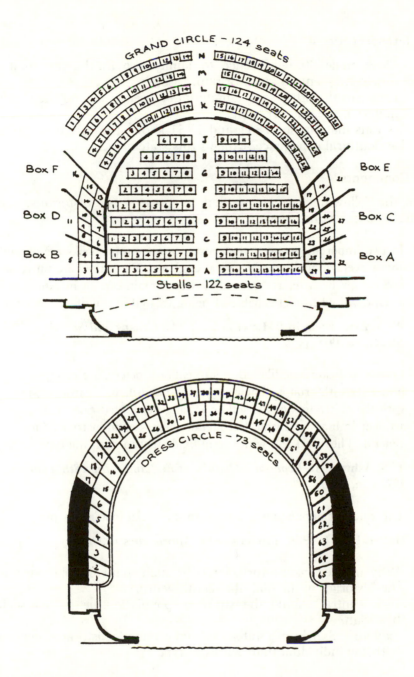

What does this exercise tell you about the nature of rank or class in a Victorian village?

C Interpretations

1 Class made little difference to family size in the first half of nineteenth-century rural Britain. Discuss.
2 How can the other source material be used to extend the Census material on Little Wratting?
3 Census material for 1841 and 1851 shows the variety of British agricultural experience. Explain this statement.

D Comments

Read the following extracts written by present-day historians, then answer the questions below.

> In two important respects the census enumerators' books are of well above average quality as historical evidence. First, they are universal and comprehensive, and secondly, they contain certain information in a standardised format capable of being treated in a uniform manner.
>
> **W. A. Armstrong in R. Lawton (ed.) *The Census and Social Structure*, 1978, p. 62**

> Economic historians, like other students of society, are concerned primarily with groups. Their subject is not Adam, a gardener, but with the cultivators of the soil as a class; not Tubal-cain, a skilled artificer in brass and iron, but metal workers or industrialists in general. They deal less with the individual than with the type. . .
>
> **T. S. Ashton, *An Economic History of England – the 18th. century*, 1972 edn, p. 17**

> The study of population is central to the social historian's purpose.
>
> **H. Perkin in H. P. R. Finberg (ed.), *Approaches to History*, 1962 p. 58**

1 Why are the census returns for 1851 such an invaluable source for the historian of the mid nineteenth century?
2 How central should the study of population be to the social historian?
3 Explain T. S. Ashton's statement that economic historians 'deal less with the individual than with the type'.

Agriculture remained the largest single male occupation in 1851 and farm workers – the 'Labs.' of the Census **[1.13(c)]** – formed the largest single occupational group. In 1831, 961 100 families were employed in farming throughout Great Britain. Of these, 144 600 were occupiers who employed labour, 130 500 were occupiers who did not employ labour and 686 000 were labouring families. These figures hide a great variety of practice and social organisation. Little Wratting is not a microcosm of mid nineteenth-century rural experience.

2 The agricultural experience – protest

This chapter examines the ways in which people living in rural England protested against their conditions. It concentrates on two specific outbreaks: one at Littleport and Ely in Cambridgeshire in 1816, and the second at Stotfold in Bedfordshire fourteen years later. Both demonstrate the basic issues over which protest occurred and the traditional ways in which that protest was expressed.

2.1 Protest nation-wide

It is a matter of history; that whilst the laurels were yet cool on the brows of our victorious soldiers on their second occupation of Paris, the elements of convulsion were at work amongst the masses of our labouring population; and that a series of disturbances commenced with the introduction of the Corn Law in 1815, and continued with   5
short intervals, until the close of the year 1816. In London and Westminster riots ensued, and were to continue for several days, whilst the bill was discussed; at Bridport, there were riots on account of the high price of bread; at Biddeford there were similar disturbances to prevent the exportation of grain; at Bury, by the   10
unemployed, to destroy machinery; at Ely, not suppressed without bloodshed; at Newcastle-on-Tyne, by colliers and others; at Glasgow, where blood was shed, on account of soup-kitchens; at Preston, by unemployed weavers; at Nottingham, by Luddites who destroyed thirty frames; at Merthyr-Tydvil, on the reduction of wages; at   15
Birmingham, by the unemployed; at Walsall, by the distressed; and December 7th 1816 at Dundee, where, owing to the high price of meal, upwards of one hundred shops were plundered.

Samuel Bamford, *Passages in the Life of a Radical*, 1844, pp. 6–7

Questions

1   Samuel Bamford was a weaver and so tends to concentrate on industrial rather than agrarian riots and protest. How is this shown in document 2.1?
2   Bamford emphasises the Corn Law of 1815. Why did its introduction cause so much anger?
3   What was the geographical distribution of disturbances in 1815–16? Show this information in an alternative form to a list.
4   What reasons does Bamford give for the disturbances? Can you identify any common thread in their causes?
5   The end of a war results in a difficult readjustment to peacetime conditions. Examine this proposition with reference to Britain between 1815 and 1820.

The disturbances that broke out in Littleport and Ely in the summer of 1816 were not isolated outbursts of discontent. They were part of a nation-wide protest against the conditions which the poorest sections of society were compelled to endure. There *may* have been some elements in common between the riots of Bridport, Newcastle and Dundee, but each part of the country had its own local conditions which led to protest. This creates problems for historians who are trying to generalise about protest at this time. Just how valid are generalisations based on a few examples?

During the year following the end of the French Wars there were riots throughout East Anglia.

2.2   Protest in East Anglia, 1816

(See map on page 64)

Questions

1   What information can you obtain from the map [2.2] about the causes of protest?
2   How can the disturbances be classified according to geographical location?
3   Why were the protests of the strong loam and clay lands of Essex, Suffolk and Norfolk different from those in the Fens?
4   The heterogeneity of demands reflects the heterogeneity of society. Discuss.

2.2 Protest in East Anglia, 1816

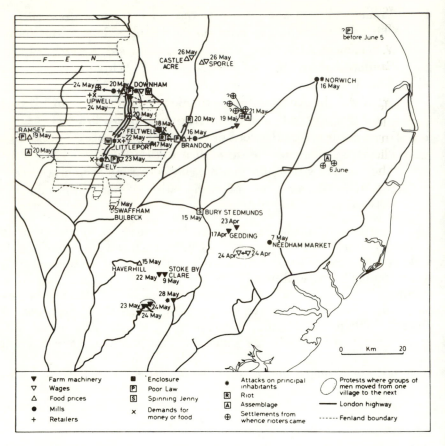

A. Charlesworth (ed.), *An Atlas of Rural Protest in Britain 1548–1900*, Croom Helm, 1983, Map 43, p. 146

The enclosure of land was often protracted and led to a great deal of simmering uncertainty.

2.3 Threat!

In Harston [near Cambridge] enclosure deprived both tenant and owners of their land. An acre was allotted to each cottage, but as most of the cottages belonged to the owners of large estates, they laid the land to them instead of attaching it to the occupiers of them, many have sold or let . . . the whole parish [Abington Pigots] 5 belonged to one person, the rights had allotments assigned them and were thrown to the farms . . . The poor are therefore greatly alarmed and view the steps taken for enclosure with terror.

W. Gooch, *General View of the Agriculture of the County of Cambridgeshire*, 1813, pp. 80–2

The effects of the Industrial Revolution caused great hardship and unemployment in East Anglia because the area had been a major centre of woollen production. New technology, particularly the threshing machine, was believed to create unemployment, though this figured much more in 1830 than in 1816. Enclosure, and the drainage of the Fens, marked a change not merely in land organisation and of crops grown but an end to the independent way of life that characterised the Fen 'Tigers'. Enclosure meant an end to livings earned by cutting the sedge and reed beds.

2.4(a) 'Want' – William Cobbett on the riots, 1816

It is want; it is sheer hunger; that is what fills a country with robbers . . . The present riots have clearly arisen out of want; out of want of food, which will make even the dumb animals break down, or leap over, fences. 'Give us food!' is the cry. 'Bread or Blood' . . . 'Tis food they want; and I know from my own observations, and have a hundred times stated the fact, that, even before this terrible distress came upon us, the labouring people had not half a sufficiency of food. 5

William Cobbett, *Political Register*, volume xxi, 8 June 1816, pp. 721–2

2.4(b)

Here I am, between Earth and Sky – so help me God. I would sooner loose my life than go home as I am. Bread I want and Bread I will have.

Evidence of William Dawson, a rioter, Cambridge Record Office Information

2.4(c)

> It was nothing to him (that many of the Littleport people had gone home) he was starved and he would be damned if he would not be fed. I might as well be hanged as starved.

> **Evidence of Richard Rutter, a rioter at Ely, Cambridge Record Office Information**

Questions

1　What evidence can be adduced from document 2.3 about the effects of enclosure in Cambridgeshire?
2　What do you understand by 'want' [2.4(a)]?
3　In what ways does William Cobbett give an incomplete explanation for the riots in 1816 [2.4(a)]? Why do you think he does this?
4　Why do William Dawson and Richard Rutter place such emphasis on 'want' [2.4(b) and 2.4(c)]?

Wages fell heavily in 1815 and unemployment increased in the Littleport area, as throughout East Anglia. The effects of this can be seen in the following documents. The first is based upon East Anglian responses to a circular sent out by the Board of Agriculture in mid 1816. The second document comes from *The Times*.

2.5

> The State of the labouring poor is very deplorable and arises entirely from the want of employment, which they are willing to seek, but the farmer cannot afford to furnish. The poor . . . they say never experienced such bad times. A parish in the next county, (without any manufacture) consisting of 3,500 acres, has, at this time, 72 men,   5 besides boys, out of employment and upon the parish . . . the labouring poor are in as bad a situation as they were in the dearth years. One third of them being out of employment, and their wages being reduced by more than another third and the price of every article of their consumption (bread excepted) being nearly equal to   10 the prices of the years 1811 and 1812.

> *The Agricultural State of England*, 1816, pp. 41, 303

2.6

> Much of the disorderly conduct of the lower orders is doubtless
> owing to the habits generated by the existing system of the poor-laws
> . . . Without a fundamental change, it is clear that the moral
> character of that peasantry which has been described as 'its country's
> pride' must be entirely destroyed; and that even the present   5
> enormous burden of eight millions annually, which the poor-rates
> impose on the industry and capital of the country, must be rapidly
> augmented.

> **The Times, 30 May 1816**

Questions

1 What does document **2.5** identify as causing unemployment and
  what does document **2.6** see as its consequence?
2 Account for the differences between documents **2.5** and **2.6**.
3 Why do you think document **2.6** expresses this particular viewpoint?
  How far do you think it represents the view in London?
4 Was there a 'moral' crisis in rural society in 1815 and 1816?

Why did riots break out at this particular time? Political scientists may
provide the answer.

2.7(a)   Alexis de Tocqueville

> So it would appear that the French found their condition the more
> unsupportable in proportion to its improvement . . . Revolutions are
> not always made by the gradual decline from bad to worse. Nations
> that have endured patiently and almost unconsciously the most
> overwhelming oppression often burst into rebellion against the yoke
> the moment it begins to grow lighter.

> **Alexis de Tocqueville, *The Old Regime and the French Revolution*,
> Fontana translation of 1856 edn, p. 214**

2.7(b) J. C. Davies

> Political stability and instability are ultimately dependent on a state of
> mind, a mood, in a society . . . It is the dissatisfied state of mind
> rather than the tangible provision of 'adequate' or 'inadequate'

supplies of food, equality or liberty which produces the revolution
. . . A revolutionary state of mind requires the continued, even   5
habitual but dynamic expectation of greater opportunity to satisfy
basic needs, which may range from merely physical (food, clothing,
shelter, health. . . .) . . . to the need for equal dignity and justice . . .
But the necessary additional ingredient is a persistent, unrelenting
threat to the satisfaction of those needs: not a threat which actually   10
returns people to the state of sheer survival but which puts them in
the mental state where they believe they will not be able to satisfy
one or more basic needs.

J. C. Davies 'Towards a theory of revolution' in *American
Sociological Review*, vol. xxvii, no.1, 1962, pp. 6–8

Questions

1   What do both de Tocqueville and Davies identify as a possible cause
     of protest [2.7(a) and 2.7(b)]?
2   What value are their conclusions to the historian attempting an
     explanation of the 1816 disturbances?
3   What explanation of protest has been advanced by Karl Marx?
4   Why should historians adopt a method which uses the ideas and
     conclusions of other disciplines?

The evidence of what happened in the Littleport riots and the subsequent
trials is surprisingly plentiful. The fullest accounts can be found in the
Treasury Solicitor's Papers, Home Office Papers held in the Public Record
Office, and in Assize records. Both the Cambridge Record Office and
Cambridge University Library contain additional information, particularly
prosecution briefs. Newspaper accounts, especially those in the *Cambridge
Chronicle* and *Journal*, are also useful. But it is perhaps only in the
confessions of those convicted that the rioters expressed themselves. In
most cases the views of the rioters were expressed through the medium of
the literate magistracy.

Questions

1   What problems do the sources pose for the historian who is trying to
     get some understanding of the experience of the rioters?
2   Most sources for rural protest in the early nineteenth century give
     the view of authority, and that was one of repression. Comment on
     this problem.

On Wednesday 22 May 1816 a group of labourers met at 'The Globe' public house. They waited unsuccessfully for men from Denver and Southery who had been involved in earlier riots and then decided to take action on their own account. They marched to the house of Revd Vachell, vicar and magistrate, to demand work and bread. He was asked to talk with local employers and had some success with one of them in negotiations held in the churchyard. Henry Martin, a leading farmer who had been overseer of the poor, promised them wages of two shillings per day and flour at two shillings and sixpence a stone. The crowd in the churchyard split and a group began rioting and robbing. Houses were ransacked and their inhabitants threatened. At about eleven o'clock that night they returned to Vachell's house where he read the Riot Act which he always kept in his hat.

2.8(a)

A desperate body of armed men had attacked the house of Mr. Vachell, a magistrate resident in Littleport, who for some time stood at his door armed with a pistol threatening to shoot anyone who should attempt to enter, when three men rushed him and disarmed him. He immediately ran upstairs to his wife and two daughters, who   5 with very slight covering made their escape with him, running nearly all the way towards Ely.

Norfolk Chronicle, 11 June 1816

They then prepared to attack Ely, choosing as their leader John Denniss, a local victualler. A farm wagon was commandeered and mounted with a punt-gun.

2.8(b)

They [the rioters] armed themselves with the most dangerous and offensive weapons, such as Bludgeons, Pitchfolks, Muck Cromes, Fork Shafts headed with short iron spikes. Fowling pieces and Fowlers' guns, the tubes of which latter are from 7 to 10 feet in length, carry about 7 lb of shot, and will kill at a distance of 150 yards.

Norfolk Chronicle, 11 June 1816

In the early hours of Thursday morning the rioters made their way to Ely, gathering support and compelling people to join them. The three magistrates in Ely were unable to persuade them to disperse and were compelled to accede to their demands. This was contained in a handbill which magistrates issued on 23 May.

2.8(c)

> The Magistrates agree and do order, that the Overseers shall pay to each poor family Two Shillings per Head per Week, when Flour is Half-a-Crown a stone, such Allowance to be raised in proportion when the Price of Flour is higher, and that the Price of Labour shall be Two Shillings per Day, whether Married or Single, and that the Labourer shall be paid his full Wages by the Farmer who Hires him. 5

> No Person to be prosecuted for any thing that has been done to the present Time; provided that every Man immediately returns peaceably to his own Home.

> **Public Record Office: Home Office Papers 42/150**

Many rioters did go home but some remained in Ely attacking shops and houses. Eventually an uneasy peace descended on the city. It was now the turn of the magistrates to act.

They sent for a troop of the First Royal Dragoons from Bury St Edmunds, and Henry Law, one of the magistrates, went to London to appeal to the Home Secretary, Viscount Sidmouth, for help. Sidmouth sent the Revd Sir Henry Bate Dudley, a canon of Ely Cathedral, back with Henry Law to pacify the area. Bate Dudley called at Royston on his way from London to collect a detachment of Yeomanry and reached Ely late on the Thursday evening. On Friday morning 24 May the military and other 'respectable gentlemen' rode to Littleport. Henry Law takes up the story.

2.8(d)

> We had no sooner reached the place than we were attacked by a most ferocious armed mob who had enclosed and barricaded themselves at the 'George' Public House. After much shooting on both sides one of our soldiers was wounded in the arm . . . and several of the rioters wounded, one of whom was killed, we succeeded in capturing fifty-six that evening. The following day forty-two were apprehended.

> **Cambridge University Library, Add. MS 4492**

This effectively ended the three days of rioting in the Fens. Major-General Sir John Byng arrived with further troops to restore order which was done with considerable efficiency and not a little brutality. The rioters' trials followed. A Special Assize was held in Ely in early to mid June 1816, presided over by the Chief Justice for the Isle of Ely, Edward Christian, brother of the leader of the mutineers on the *Bounty*. Of the fifty-three rioters brought to trial, twenty-four received capital sentences. However, nineteen had their sentences commuted to varying degrees of transportation. The remaining five – John Denniss, William Beamiss, Thomas South, George Crow and Isaac Harley – were executed on Friday 28 June 1816.

Questions

Use this narrative and the documents [2.8(a), (b), (c) and (d)] to answer the following questions.

1   What was the initial response of 'the authorities' to the rioters' threats?
2   How organised were the rioters?
3   What characteristic features of riots in agrarian areas can be identified from this example?
4   Maintaining public order was ultimately the responsibility of the military in the early nineteenth century. Why?
5   There was a lack of gentry in the Fens. If there had been more men of authority to organise effective action against demonstrations a dramatic breakdown of law and order could probably have been avoided. Discuss.
6   Central government could not support local concessions by magistrates. Why?

Were the Littleport and Ely riots part of a general conspiracy in East Anglia? William Hobhouse, a Treasury Solicitor whose duty it was to prepare the prosecution of the rioters, certainly thought so:

2.9

> A settled plan of disorder, of rapine and violence, seems to have been formed, and carried into execution; partly too, by men who were in none of the situations . . . and for whose conduct therefore no strong justification on the grounds of absolute want can be pleaded . . .
> Many of the most conspicuous actors in the dark drama were persons 5
> above the lowest classes of society, persons who were not compelled

to earn their hard morsel by their daily labour, but persons who possessed some property and something like an aspect of reputation. Their motives must have been more than ordinarily malignant

William Hobhouse, printed in C. Johnson, *The Ely and Littleport Riots*, 1893, pp. 10–11

Questions

1   Is William Hobhouse using facts or rhetoric in this passage [2.9]?
2   What evidence does Hobhouse give for his idea of a general conspiracy?
3   What advantages did the 'authorities' gain from stressing the idea of conspiracy?
4   Repression by the 'authorities' was underpinned by their fear of revolution. Discuss.

Who were the rioters and what occupational groups did they come from? Examine document 2.10, a list of rioters drawn up for the Treasury Solicitors in 1816.

2.10

Rioters in prison

	A	B	C	D	E	F	G	H	I
1.	Wm Atkin		Ely		2		4		
2.	Wm Beamiss sen.	M	L	Shoemaker	4				
3.	Wm Beamiss jun.	S	L	"	3				
4.	Chris Butcher		L	Labourer	1				
5.	John Burridge	S	L	"	2			4/-	
6.	Richard Burridge	M	L	"	1		1	£1	
7.	Mark Benton	M	L	"	2		1	£1	
8.	Henry Benson	M	L	Farmer	1	Claimed authorship			
9.	Richard Burridge		L	Labourer	5				
10.	James Cammell	M	L	"	3		3		
11.	Hy Chapman		Ely	"	2				
12.	Aaron Chevall	M	L	"	4		5	15/-	
13.	Robt Crabb	M	L	"	2		2	10/-	
14.	Jarvis Cranwell	M	L	"	1				
15.	Richard Cooper		Ely	No job	1	Riot at Ely / Very active			
16.	John Cooper		Ely	Brickmaker	1	" "			
17.	Rich Cooper jun.		Ely	No job	1	" "			
18.	Geo Crow	M	L	Labourer	3	At least		8/-	
19.	John Denniss	M	L	Victualler	3				
20.	Wm Dann	M	L	Labourer	3		5	15/-	
21.	Thos Dobbs	M	L	"	1		2	12/-	
22.	Thos Dench		Ely	"	1				
23.	Joseph Easey	M	L	"	3		1	9/-	2/-

	A	B	C	D	E	F	G	H	I
24.	John Easey	M	L	"	2		1	9/-	
25.	Thos Edgerley		Ramsey	Waterman	1		3	14/-	
26.	John Freeman	M	L	Labourer	1		4	12/-	
27.	John Gaultrip	M	L	"	1		3	12/-	
28.	Thos Gray	M	L	Shoemaker	1			9/-	4/6
29.	John Green	S	L	Labourer	2			9/-	
30.	Wm Gotobed	M	L	"	1				
31.	Thos Gotobed				1	Not apprehended			
32.	Wm Greaves		No place	"	1				
33.	Flanders Hopkin		Downham	"	2				
34.	Thos Hunt	M	L	Tailor	1		4	9/-	2/6
35.	John Hunt	M	Ely	Labourer	1	Very active		9/-	
36.	Isaac Harley jun.	M	L	"	3		2		
37.	Sarah Hobbes		Ely	"	1				
38.	Joseph Hopkins		Downham		1	Not apprehended			
39.	John Hassett			'Irishman'					
40.	Richard Jessop	M	L	Labourer	6		1	9/-	
41.	Joseph Irons		L	"		Bail			
42.	John Lee	M	L	"	1	Bailed	3	14/-	
43.	Aaron Layton		Ely	Bricklayer	2				
44.	Jos Lavender	M	L	Labourer	1		3	10/-	8d
45.	Wm Murfitt	M	L	"	1		1	9/-	
46.	Hy Mainer	S	L	"	4			6/-	
47.	John Morris	M	L	Shoemaker	1			9/-	
48.	Philip Morris	M	L	Labourer					
49.	Eliz Newman	S	L	Single woman	1		1		5/-
50.	Robt Nicholas	S	L	Labourer	1	Active		9/-	
51.	Jas Newall	S	L	"	1			8/-	

No.	Name			Occupation		Notes			
52.	Rich Nicholas	S	L	"	2			6/-	
53.	Robt Porter	S	L	"	1			9/-	
54.	John Pricke		Ely	Potter	1			9/-	
55.	Rich Rutter	M	L	Labourer	1		1		
56.	Stephen Rowell	M	L	"	1		3	12/-	
57.	Brassett Rayner	M	L	Shopkeeper	1	Treasurer / Occupier of land of his own			1/6
58.	Jos Stibbard	S	L	Labourer	1	Chelsea Pensioner		8/-	
59.	Samuel Seakins		Downham	"	1				
60.	Matthew Seakins		"	"	1				
61.	Thos Seakins		"	"	1			6/-	
62.	Thos South jun.	S	L	"	10			6/-	
63.	Robert Salmon	S	L	"	3			10/-	
64.	Wm Sibley	M	L	Carpenter	1		2	15/-	
65.	David Stimson				1	Secreting rioters			
66.	John Sparrow	S			1	Crown witness			
67.	John South	S							
68.	John Jefferson	S	L	Labourer				6/-	
69.	Wm Jefferson	S	L	"				9/-	
70.	Robt Porter	S						9/-	
71.	Francis Torrington	S	L	Shoemaker	1	Pension: Marine Service		9/-	1/3
72.	Jas Worthy	M	L	Labourer	1		4	10/-	
73.	Wm Walker	S	L	"	2			8/-	
74.	Wm Wilson		Downham	Shoemaker	2			12/-	
75.	John Walton		Ely	"	1				
76.	John Wilson		Downham		1				
77.	Daniel Wilson	M	L	Blacksmith	2	In business for himself	3		

	A	B	C	D	E	F	G	H	I
78.	John Warner	M	L	Labourer	1			9/-	
79.	Wilson Wyebrow	M	L				1	9/-	
80.	John Walker	M	L	,,			3	10/-	

Key to Table

A – name of labourer

B – married or single

C – village

D – occupation

E – number of offences

F – remarks

G – number of children

H – average weekly earnings* (though in general these are lower than the weekly earnings of the Prisoners' families as they do not take other family earnings into account – in many cases the earnings of the women and children could not be ascertained)

I – weekly allowance from Parish*

L – Littleport

* Amounts in pounds, shillings and pence (£/s/d); 12d = 1s (5p), 20s = £1 (100p)

From the Treasury Solicitors, 1816, printed in A. J. Peacock, *Bread and Blood: a study of the Agrarian Riots in East Anglia in 1816*, Gollancz 1965, pp. 174–6

Questions

1   In what other forms is it possible to show the information in the table [2.10]?
2   What information can be learned about the rioters from document **2.10**?
3   What hypotheses can you construct about the social character of rural protest from this evidence? Assess their validity.
4   How far did occupation in rural society determine attitudes to protest in the early nineteenth century?

Although the Littleport and Ely riots were concerned primarily with 'bread and butter' issues there was an implied call for 'justice' and a restoration of the 'moral' economy. Labourers only acted on a large scale when conditions became really intolerable and only then did they have any national impact. However, a close examination of the local press gives a different story, one of local impact. Labourers were experts in slacking in highly effective and almost indetectable ways. More seriously, they could steal their employers' corn, fruit and game despite the severity of the sentence if caught. Sheep and horse stealing were capital offences until 1831 and arson remained so until 1837. Poaching was endemic in rural areas. Stacks could be fired, farm buildings lit, fences pulled down, animals maimed and drainage channels breached.

2.11(a)

> Agrarian outrages are very frequent occurrences in the neighbourhood of Ely: two or three times the crier is employed every week to announce some destruction of someone's property. The farmers complain of their fences being broken down, and pigeons being shot: within a few days Mr James Cheesewright had his potato   5
> heap robbed three times, and on Wednesday evening last all of the potatoes of Mr Mark Manchet were stolen from out of his pit. Offering rewards proves . . . useless . . . in bringing the parties to punishment.
>
> *Cambridge Chronicle*, 13 January 1844

2.11(b) An arson letter

> Mr. Watkin, Sir – This come as a warnin for you and the police, it is the entenshun if an alterantion is not made verry wuick you shall

have a totch of Carlton [a neighbouring village where there had been
fires] for wee hav prepared ourselves for you all. i understand you
have got a wheat hoe and we have got a life-hoe prepared for you and   5
not you alone, but you will be the first if you do not make an
alterashun, we will make an exampel of you enstead of your making
an exampel for the pore to be kept alive, your Exampel is, to have
them all starved to death you damnd raskell. You bluddy farmers
could not liv if it was not for the poore, tis them that keep you   10
bluddy raskells alive, but there will be a slauter made amonst you
very soone. I shood verry well like to hang you the same as I hanged
your beastes. You bluddy rogue, I will lite up a little fire for you the
first opportunity that I can make, and I shood like to have their at
the present time. If the pore be not employed differed to what they   15
have bin, it shall be as the promes is made.

**Letter written by Edmund Botwright, tried for arson at the Suffolk
Assizes in 1844, printed in the *Cambridge Chronicle*, 3 August 1844**

2.11(c) Last words

Good bye, good bye and God bless you all – I hope my fate will be a
warning to you all, and I hope you gentlemen farmers will give the
young men work; it was the want of work that brought me to this.

**George Pulham (aged 22), on the scaffold in 1835, printed in the
Cambridge Chronicle, 17 April 1835**

2.11(d)

23 November 1832
Elm. Three stacks of oats fired. 'There is no doubt but that it is the
work of an incendiary.'

30 November 1832
Elm Stacks belonging to William Dow burnt. 'During the time the   5
engine was playing upon the fire, one of the pipes was cut.'

14 December 1832
Upwell. Fifth attempt to fire the corn stacks of Thomas Wiles.

1 March 1833
On Saturday 17 February two banks belonging to the North Level 10
Commissioners were cut, Wednesday, 'a dam which protects the farm
of Mr John Marshall's from the innundation of the Old Elm Leam
was cut through which did very great damage to his property.'

4 October 1833
'The midnight sheep-slaughterer has been at work again in the Parish 15
of Elm. On Saturday last, Mr John Dow, who, we have before
recorded as a sufferer, lost a valuable wether.'

7 November 1834
Wisbech. 'The system of thieving in this neighbourhood seems to be
so well organised that nothing comes amiss or to have any 20
apprehension of detection.' 28 fleeces of wool taken at West Walton.

From the *Cambridge Chronicle*, 1832–4; an extended list is printed
in J. P. D. Dunbadin (ed.), *Rural Discontent in Nineteenth Century
Britain*, 1974, pp. 40–3

Questions

1   From extracts **2.11(a)–(d)** construct a typology of the different ways
    in which the agricultural labourer could protest.
2   What was the labourer protesting against?
3   Social protest or crime? How is it possible to distinguish between the
    two in these extracts?
4   Emphasis by historians upon 1816, 1822 and 1830 has given the
    impression of the failure of social protest. In fact throughout this
    period rural Britain was a potential powder keg. Discuss.

There had been sporadic unrest in Bedfordshire since 1815 which reached
a peak in 1828 and 1829, culminating in the Stotfold riots of 1830. Are
there any differences between the 1816 riots and those in Stotfold fourteen
years later? Unemployment and the necessity for parish relief were again
important reasons for unrest which largely took the form of damage to
property. For example, in January 1827 four Shillington men were given
the alternative of a fine, or three months imprisonment for wilfully
damaging parish wheelbarrows.

In 1830, however, the scale of protest took on a new and, from the point
of view of the landowners, highly threatening dimension. The 'Swing' riots

began in June. They became known as such because of the anonymous letters addressed to landowners, often signed 'Captain Swing', threatening arson and the destruction of farm machinery. The first threshing machines were attacked near Canterbury on 28 August and by the end of October about a hundred had been destroyed. But the riots were more than just attacks on machines; labourers assembled to demand higher rates of pay, rent reductions, tax and tithe reform – 'bargaining by riots'. By the end of November more or less the whole of southern and eastern England was affected.

There were no examples of machine breaking in Bedfordshire but on 11 November 1830 the first case of arson took place near Holcutt. A further case was reported at Wotton Phillinge on 27 November. The *Northampton Mercury* reported on 4 December that 'no threshing machine was used on the farm' but ended ominously that 'several persons have received threatening letters with the signature 'Swing'. The best documented disturbance took place at Stotfold on 2 December.

2.12(a) Arson

THE HOME OF THE RICK-BURNER.

Punch, 1830

2.12(b)   Beginnings

Late on Wednesday evening, the labourers began to assemble
together, and many of the more peaceable inhabitants were forcibly
dragged from their beds and compelled to join the rabble. They then
proceeded to the residences of the more respectable inhabitants and
demanded an increase in wages and on being told that their   5
complaints would be dealt with by the vestry at 10 a.m. the following
morning they dispersed. But long before daylight in the morning they
collected again and proceeded to every farm house in the village and
compelled every man and boy that was willing to work to join them.

***Northampton Mercury*, 4 December 1830**

2.12(c)   Vestry meeting

They then demanded, first, to be wholly exempt from the payment of
taxes. This was agreed to. They next demanded the dismissal of the
assistant overseer. This was also agreed to. Then they required that
every man should receive 2 shillings per day for his work.

***The Times*, 4 December 1830**

2.12(d)   Bargaining by riot

Late in the evening they separated, hinting, that if their wishes were
not granted on Saturday, they would on that evening have recourse to
further violence. On the Friday they resumed their labours; but a
meeting of the principal inhabitants was held in the afternoon . . .
and a communication of the circumstances was made to W. H.   5
Whitbread, Esq. the magistrate, who took immediate measures for the
apprehension of the ringleaders . . . the magistrate proceeded to
Stotfold, and in little more than half an hour, ten leaders were taken,
and forthwith committed to the country gaol.

***The Times*, 4 December 1830**

A slightly different account of the proceedings is given in the letters from
John Lafont, curate of Stotfold and Hertfordshire magistrate to Lord
Grantham, Lord Lieutenant of Bedfordshire.

2.12(e)   The Lafont letters

4 December. Things are in such a state at Stotfold in this county that
I thought it right to ride over to your lordship's house . . . I have
since come back again to Silsoe, having seen Mr Whitbread and Mr
Edwards of Henlow, and am now with their concurrence desiring 50
of your lordship's men to assemble and proceed forthwith. I do not   5
apprehend serious resistance if we are there before dark. We want to
take into custody the ringleader of Thursday last. I am a
Hertfordshire magistrate and rector of Hinxworth, the parish
adjoining Stotfold, and unless these men are taken tonight the
consequences tomorrow in the neighbourhood parishes may be   10
dreadful.

5 December . . . It was late on Friday night before I was acquainted
with the revolutionary proceedings in Bedfordshire of Thursday. It
struck me at once as essential for the general good that a blow be
struck at Stotfold before dark on Saturday; on which morning . . . [I] 15
proceeded to Henlow to consult Mr Edwards. I proposed to him that
I should gallop back immediately and muster your lordship's men; of
this he highly approved and the result was that 120 of your excellent
fellows were at the point required by 3 o'clock . . . The Parish of
Stotfold, mustering 300 men and boys, was in perfect tranquillity all   20
night, instead of being in positive revolt; and this day, Sunday, men
were touching their hats to their masters who never did so in their
lives before. We took 10 of the ringleaders – only one escaped . . . If
we had not put Stotfold down on Saturday, a coalition of perhaps
2,000 men would have been effected within 24 hours . . . All the   25
threshing machines hereabouts have been pulled down by their
owners, added to which the farmers have been so far intimidated as
to raise their wages generally, without satisfying them. There is a fire
now burning within 10 miles of this place, supposed to be near
Royston. On Thursday night there were four within sight from the   30
high ground two miles off.

Bedfordshire Record Office L30/18/27/1–2

Questions

1   Using the sources above [2.12(a)–(e)] write an account showing what
     happened at Stotfold early in December 1830.

2   Explain the discrepancies between Lafont's letters [2.12(e)] and the other evidence.
3   When calls for justice and for order came into conflict it was order that won. Discuss this proposition in relation to the Stotfold riots.
4   Compare and contrast the Littleport and Ely riots with those at Stotfold.

These incidents of rural radicalism must be seen against the whole background of poverty and the general hopelessness of over-population and under-employment. It was a lack of understanding of the character of change, both by labourers and their employers, that contributed largely to the increased incidence of rural protest in the early to mid nineteenth century. Change imperfectly understood aroused fear which was often fanned by rumour. This was made worse by want. As Lord Bacon wrote in his submission to the Poor Law Royal Commission in 1834,

> The surest way to prevent sedition, if the times do bear it, is to take away the matter of them . . . the rebellions of the belly are worst.

3 The industrial experience

Between 1800 and 1850 there were many changes in British industry. What exactly were these changes and how dramatic were they? Emphasis has been placed both by contemporaries and by later historians on the changes in organisation and location of textile production, especially in cotton and woollen production. But capitalist methods of production predated industrial changes. Out-working was not the only way of manufacturing goods. Mining, for example, could never be organised in that way.

3.1(a)

I visited England for the first time 52 years ago . . . to judge how far and how completely . . . industrial activity had developed, as against that which the Continent could show; and I must confess that the verdict fell entirely in favour of England . . . Yet nothing very new could be observed there at that period . . . the same things were to be   5
found elsewhere, though not so good . . . Twenty years later . . . I found great new developments in the above mentioned field. Spinning mills, foundries, potteries . . . steel and file factories, the plating works of Birmingham and Sheffield, the spinning and weaving mills of Manchester, and the cloth manufacture of Leeds,   10
had acquired a size and perfection of which there can be no conception without actually seeing them . . . Twelve or thirteen years later . . . the scale of everything and especially the expansion of London had increased yet more . . . The already extensive steam navigation, the general installation of gas lighting, Perkin's steam-   15
driven shuttles, Brunel's great tunnel . . . besides much else of the greater interest . . . remain in my mind . . . as an ever fascinating picture.

Johann Conrad Fischer, Diary, 1851

3.1(b)

It is of some importance at what period a man is born. A young man, alive at this period, hardly knows to what improvements of human life he has been introduced; and I would like to bring before his notice the following . . . changes which have taken place since I first began to breathe . . . Gas was unknown: I groped about the streets of 5 London in all but the utter darkness of a twinkling oil lamp, under the protection of watchmen . . . and exposed to every species of depredation and insult.

I have been nine hours in sailing from Dover to Calais before the invention of steam. It took me nine hours to go from Taunton to 10 Bath, before the invention of steam-roads, and I now go in six hours from Taunton to London! In going from Taunton to Bath, I suffered between 10,000 and 12,000 contusions before stone-breaking Macadam was born.

I can walk, by the assistance of the police, without molestation; or, 15 if tired, get into a cheap and active cab . . . The corruptions of Parliament, before Reform, infamous . . . The Poor laws were gradually sapping the vitals of the country; and, whatever miseries I suffered, I had no post to whisk my complaints for a single penny to the remotest corners of the empire.

From 'Modern Changes' in *Collected Works of the Reverend Sydney Smith*, 1839

Questions

1   What evidence of industrial change did Johann Fischer and Sydney Smith identify [3.1(a) and (b)]?
2   How does the emphasis of the two documents differ? Account for this.
3   How had Britain's cities become safer and communication been improved according to Smith [3.1(b)]? Assess his judgement.

The changes in the economy led to changes in employment, as Robert Owen wrote in 1815:

3.2

Those who are engaged in the trade, manufactures, and commerce of this country thirty or forty years ago formed but a very insignificant portion of the knowledge, wealth, influence or population of the Empire.

Prior to that period, Britain was essentially agricultural. But, from   5
that time to the present, the home and foreign trade have increased in
a manner so rapid and extraordinary as to have raised commerce to
an importance, which it never previously attained in any country
possessing so much political power and influence.

(By the returns to the Population Act in 1811, it appears that in   10
England, Scotland and Wales there are 895,998 families chiefly
employed in agriculture – 1,129,049 families chiefly employed in
trade and manufactures – 640,500 individuals in the army and navy –
and 519,168 families not engaged in any of these employments. It
follows that nearly half as many more persons are engaged in trade as   15
in agriculture – and that of the whole population the agriculturists
are about 1 to 3.)

This change has been owing chiefly to the mechanical inventions
which introduced the cotton trade into this country, and to the
cultivation of the cotton tree in America . . . The general diffusion of   20
manufactures throughout a country generates a new character in its
inhabitants; and as this character is formed upon a principle quite
unfavourable to individual or general happiness, it will produce the
most lamentable and permanent evils, unless its tendency be
counteracted by legislative interference and direction . . . This   25
alteration is still in rapid progress; and ere long, the comparatively
happy simplicity of the agricultural peasant will be wholly lost among
us. It is even now scarcely anywhere to be found without a mixture
of those habits which are the offspring of trade, manufactures and
commerce.

'Observations on the Effects of the Manufacturing System', 1815, in
Robert Owen, *A New View of Society and other writings*, Dent 1972,
pp. 120–1

Questions

1   What did Robert Owen identify as the cause of changes in
     employment [3.2]? How simplistic do you find this view?
2   Assess Owen's analysis of the consequences of these changes.
3   It was not just the changes in employment but their increasingly
     urban location which caused major problems. Discuss.
4   How far was Owen's analysis of industrialisation the result of his
     own commercial experience?

3.3(a)   Distribution of the British labour force in various occupations 1801–51 (in millions, and as a percentage of the total work-force)

Agriculture, forestry, fishing

	Millions	Percentage of total
1801	1.7	35.9
1811	1.8	33.0
1821	1.8	28.4
1831	1.8	24.6
1841	1.9	22.2
1851	2.1	21.7

Manufacture, mining, industry

	Millions	Percentage of total
1801	1.4	27.9
1811	1.7	30.2
1821	2.4	38.4
1831	3.0	40.8
1841	3.3	40.5
1851	4.1	42.9

Trade, transport

	Millions	Percentage of total
1801	0.5	11.2
1811	0.6	11.6
1821	0.8	12.1
1831	0.9	12.4
1841	1.2	14.2
1851	1.5	15.8

Domestic, personal service

	Millions	Percentage of total
1801	0.6	11.5
1811	0.7	11.8
1821	0.8	12.7
1831	0.9	12.6
1841	1.2	14.5
1851	1.3	13.0

Public, professional service

	Millions	Percentage of total
1801	0.3	11.8
1811	0.4	13.3
1821	0.3	8.5
1831	0.3	9.5
1841	0.3	8.5
1851	0.5	6.7

Based on P. Deane and W. A. Cole, *British Economic Growth 1688–1959*, CUP, 1964, pp. 142–3

3.3(b)

Major occupations of the work-force in England and Wales (in thousands)

	No. of men (in thousands)		No. of women (in thousands)		Total
	1–19	20+	1–19	20+	
Commerce Trade Manufacture	318	1750	159	391	2618
Agriculture	162	1042	9	48	1261
Domestic service	84	150	289	476	999
Living on means	5	119	14	308	446
Total occupied	724	4062	505	1416	6707
Total unoccupied	2936	239	3157	3059	9391

Based upon the 1841 Census, England and Wales

3.3(c)

Numbers employed in various occupations in the major trades in England and Wales (30 000+) in 1851 (in thousands)

Agricultural labourer, farm servant, shepherd	1461
Domestic servant	1039
Cotton calico manufacturer, printing, dyeing	502
Labourer (undefined)	377
Farmer, grazier	307
Boot and shoe maker	274
Milliner, dressmaker	268
Coal-miner	219
Carpenter, joiner	183
Army, navy	179
Tailor	153
Washerwoman, mangler	146
Woollen cloth manufacturer	138
Silk manufacturer	115
Blacksmith	113
Worsted manufacturer	104
Mason, pavior	101
Messenger, porter, errand boy	101
Linen manufacturer	99
Seaman (at home)	89
Grocer	86
Gardener	81
Iron manufacturer	80

Innkeeper, licensed victualler, beershop keeper	76
Seamstress, shirtmaker	73
Bricklayer	68
Butcher, meat salesman	68
Hose manufacturer	65
School master/mistress	65
Lace manufacturer	64
Plumber, painter, glazier	63
Baker	62
Carman, carrier, carter	57
Charwoman	55
Draper	49
Engine/machine maker	48
Commercial clerk	44
Cabinet maker	41
Teacher (various), governess	41
Fisherman/woman	41
Boat/barge/man/woman	38
Miller	37
Earthenware manufacturer	37
Sawyer	35
Railway labourer	34
Straw-plait manufacturer	32
Brickmaker/dealer	31
Government Civil Service	31
Hawker/pedlar	31
Wheelwright	30

Based upon the 1851 Census, England and Wales.

Questions

1   What major changes in the distribution of employment can be identified in document **3.3(a)**? Account for these changes.
2   How can the information in document **3.3(b)** be shown graphically?
3   Explain the differences between male and female employment in 1841 [**3.3(b)**].
4   Using document **3.3(c)** produce a classification of occupations.
5   Occupations which manufactured things were far less important in 1851 than many people believed. Discuss this in relation to document **3.3(c)**.
6   Economic change led to a down–grading of certain crafts and skills. Assess this statement.

There was a diversity of people and trades by 1851 just as there had been in 1800. There was still a sharp division between artisans and the journeymen who were serving their apprenticeship. In traditional trades – many of which not only survived but grew – the position of the artisan remained little changed. The creation of new skills during the Industrial Revolution led to the gradual growth of new elites – foremen, overseers, mechanics and technicians as well as managers. But increasingly it was the distinction between skilled and unskilled, or general labourers, which was to have most economic and social significance.

Myth has played an important part in historians' views of these changes. The factory symbolised the new methods of production and yet most people worked for very small employers. Even in the cotton industry only 41 out of a total of 1670 in 1851 employed more than one hundred people. Steam power was not introduced as quickly as once thought. What about the issue of child labour?

3.4(a)   Robert Owen on child labour

Not more than thirty years since, the poorest parents thought the age of fourteen sufficiently early for their children to commence regular labour: and they judged well; for by that period of their lives they had acquired by play and exercise in the open air, the foundation of a sound robust constitution; and if they were not all initiated in book   5
learning, they had been taught the far more useful knowledge of domestic life, which could not but be familiar to them at the age of fourteen, and which, as they grew up and became heads of families, was of more value to them (as it taught them economy in the expenditure of their earnings) than one half of their wages under   10
present circumstances . . . Contrast this state of affairs with that of the lower orders of the present day . . . In the manufacturing districts it is common for parents to send their children of both sexes at seven or eight years of age, in winter as well as summer, at six o'clock in the morning, sometimes of course in the dark, and   15
occasionally amidst frost and snow, to enter the manufactories, which are often heated to a high temperature, and contain an atmosphere far from being the most favourable to human life, and in which all those employed in them very frequently continue until twelve o'clock at noon, when an hour is allowed for dinner, after which they return to   20
remain, in a majority of cases, till eight o'clock at night . . . The direct object of these observations is to effect the amelioration and

avert the danger. The only mode by which these objects can be accomplished is to obtain an Act of Parliament . . .

To prevent children from being employed in mills of machinery   25
until they shall be ten years old, or that they shall not be employed
more than six hours per day until they shall be twelve years old . . .
Parents who have grown up in ignorance and bad habits, and who
consequently are in poverty may say 'We cannot afford to maintain
our children until they shall be twelve years of age without putting   30
them into employment by which they may earn wages, and we
therefore object to that part of the plan which precludes us from
sending them to manufactories until they shall be of that age.'

**'Observations on the Effects of the Manufacturing System', 1815, in
Robert Owen, *A New View of Society and other writings*, Dent 1972,
pp. 123–5**

3.4(b)

Mr — remarked that nothing could be so beneficial to a country as
manufactures. 'You see these children, sir' said he. 'In most parts of
England poor children are a burthen to their parents and to the
parish; here the parish, which would else have to support them, is rid
of all expense; they get their bread almost as soon as they can run   5
about, and by the time they are seven or eight years old bring in
money. There is no idleness among us – they come at five in the
morning; we allow them half an hour for breakfast, and an hour for
dinner; they leave work at six, and another set relieves them for the
night; the wheels never stand still.' I was looking, while he spoke, at   10
the unnatural dexterity with which the fingers of these little creatures
were playing in the machinery, half giddy myself with the noise and
the endless motion; and when he told me there was no rest in these
walls, day or night, I thought that if Dante had peopled one of his
hells with children, here was a scene worthy to have supplied him   15
with new images of torment.

Robert Southey, *Letters from England*, 1807

Questions

1   What justification for the widespread use of child labour did Robert
Owen and Robert Southey have to contend with?

2   What were the results of child labour according to Owen [3.4(a)]?
     How is his interpretation different from Southey's [3.4(b)]?
3   Owen's solution to the problem was legislation. Why did this prove
     difficult?
4   In what ways was there a difference between the 'free' child and the
     pauper apprentice? What difference did this make when it came to
     child labour?

But child labour and its abuse predated the Industrial Revolution.

3.5   An earlier response

A most unhappy practice prevails in most places to apprentice poor
children, no matter to what master provided he lives out of the
parish; if the child serves the first forty days we are rid of him for
ever. The master may be a tiger in cruelty; he may beat, abuse, strip
naked, starve, or do what he will to the poor innocent lad . . . I knew   5
a poor old weaver . . . who some time ago took a poor apprentice
from another parish; he covenanted, as is usual, to teach him his
trade, to provide and allow him meat, drink, apparel, etc. to save
harmless and indemnify the parish whence he took him, and to give
him two good suits of wearing apparel at the end of his   10
apprenticeship . . . as soon as the money he had with the boy was
spent threw himself, apprentice and all, upon the parish . . .

Anon., *Enquiry into the Causes of the Increase of the Poor*, 1738,
p. 43

Questions

1   What similarities are there between documents 3.4(a) and (b) and
     document 3.5? What differences are there?
2   How bad were conditions for 'pauper' labour in the eighteenth
     century? How did the 1802 Health and Morals of Apprentices Act
     improve conditions?

The reduction in child labour in the first half of the nineteenth century was
to some extent a result of legislation. But by 1850 control had been
extended only to textiles and mining.

3.6 Numbers of boys and girls (under fifteen) employed in various occupations in Britain, 1851

Boys

Occupation	No. in thousands	Percentage of total employed
Agriculture	120	28.4
Textiles	82	19.4
Navigation and docks	46	10.9
Mines	37	8.7
Metal workers*	26	6.1
Dress	23	5.4
General labour	15	3.5
Dealing (various)**	12	2.8
Building	11	2.6
Domestic service	9	2.1
Earthenware	6	1.4
Others	36	8.5
Total employed	423	

Girls

Occupation	No. in thousands	Percentage of total employed
Textiles	98	41.3
Domestic service	71	30.0
Dress	32	13.5
Agriculture	17	7.2
Metal workers*	4	1.7
Navigation and docks	4	1.7
Earthenware	3	1.3
Dealing (various)**	2	0.8
Others	6	2.5
Total employed	237	

* including those in the manufacture of machinery and tools
** including those employed in lodging and coffee houses

Based on C. Booth in 'Occupations of the People of the United Kingdom 1801–1881', *Journal of the Royal Statistical Society,* **vol. xlix, 1886**

Questions

1   Explain the major differences between the occupations of boys and girls in 1851 [3.6].
2   The employment of boys was more important than that of girls. Does document **3.6** substantiate this?
3   'The proportion of children in the population was considerably larger than it is today, so the burden that would be placed upon the rest of the community by completely withdrawing children from the labour force was very great indeed.' (E. H. Hunt *British Labour History 1815–1914*, 1981, p. 10) Discuss.
4   Why was child employment in the cotton mills singled out for regulation?
5   Discuss the argument that working conditions for children were better in the first half of the nineteenth century than the last half of the eighteenth.
6   Emphasis on conditions in mines and factories directed attention away from other major areas of child labour and abuse. Discuss.

The documents in the final part of this chapter examine the ways in which a small industrial community changed between 1823 and 1848. This will be done by a comparison between entries in the *Yorkshire Directory* in those two years.

3.7(a)   Haworth in 1823

Haworth, in the parish of Bradford, wapentake of Morley, and honour of Pontefract; 4 miles S. of Keighley. Population 4663.

Bronte, Rev. Patrick, curate
Oddy, Rev. Miles
Balfield, John, gentleman
Ackroyd, Thomas, victualler, Sun
    (Inn)
Andrew, Thomas, surgeon
Barraclough, George, ironmonger
    and watch maker
Bottomly, George, stone mason

Corlake, George, vict. Old King's
    Arms
Craven and Murgatroyd, corn mill
    millers
Harnett, Wm. Vict. White Lion
Hartley, Wm. brazier and tinner
Jowitt, Jonathan, whitesmith
Midgely, Wm., vict. Fleece
Ramsden and Co., plasterers
Thomas, Wm., spirit merchant
Townsend, G. and W., worsted
    spinners
Wilkinson, Abraham, victualler,
    Black Bull
Wood, John, plumber and glazier
Wright, Wm., vict., Hope and
    Anchor
Wright, Nathaniel, worsted yarn
    mfcturer.
Wright and Newsome, cotton spin-
    ners and manufacturers

Butchers
Midgley, Robert
Rushforth, Abraham
Storey, John
Thomas, Wm.
Thomas, John

Cabinet makers
Greenwood, John
Soper, John
Sugden, Abm.

Confectioners
Kaye, David
Rushforth, Abm.

Grocers, etc.
Atkinson, Henry
Barraclough, Jas.
Barraclough, Fra.
Driver, Jas.
Hartley, John
Hartley, Timothy
Lambert, Tobias
Pickles, William
Thomas, John
Wood, John
Wright, James

Woolstaplers
Eccles, William
Sutcliffe, Joseph
Townend, W. J. and J.

Pickles, Robert
Sugden, and Heaton
Townend, E. and W.

Worsted mfrs.
Feather Brothers
Greenwood, James

Worsted top mfrs.
Craven, Uriah
Staincliffe, Wm.

3.7(b)   Haworth in 1848

HAWORTH, a large old village, 4 miles S. by W. of Keighley, embosomed in the high moorlands, has in its own township and chapelry the hamlets of STANBURY, 1 mile W.; and NEAR and FAR OXENHHOPE, from 1 to 3 miles south of Haworth; and many scattered houses, &c. The township contains 6848 souls, and 10,540   5
acres of land, stretching westward to the borders of Lancashire, and nearly half of it in uncultivated heaths and commons. The MANORS and their owners are–*Haworth*, W. B. Ferrand, Esq.; *Oxenhope*, Joseph Greenwood, Esq.; and *Stanbury*, the Misses Rawson. Two *cattle fairs* are held at Haworth, on Easter Monday and the Monday   10
after Old Michaelmas day. *Haworth Church* (St. Michael) was rebuilt in the reign of Henry VIII., and enlarged in 1755. The perpetual curacy, valued at £170, is in the gift of the vicar of Bradford, and incumbency of the Rev. P. Bronte, B.A. *Oxenhope Church* (St. Mary) was built in 1849, at the cost of £1500, and is a perpetual curacy,   15
valued at £150, in the alternate patronage of the Crown and the Bishop of Ripon. *Stanbury Curacy*, valued at £100, is in the gift of the incumbent of Haworth. The Wesleyans have three, the Primitive Methodists one, and the Baptists two chapels, in the township. The *Free School at Haworth* is endowed with about £90, and that at   20
Stanbury with about £30 a year.

POST OFFICES, at Wm. Hartley's, *Haworth*; Wm. Whitaker's, *Far Oxenhope*; and Abm. Sunderland's, *Stanbury*. Letters despatched 3 aft. *via* Keighley.

Marked 1, reside at Near Oxenhope; 2, Far Oxenhope; 3, Stanbury; &
   the rest in Haworth.
Akroyd, Jonathan, woolstapler
2 Bankroft Timothy, surveyor, &c.
Barraclough Zbbl. ironmonger
Bronte Rev Patrick, B.A. incumbent of Haworth
Crabtree Jph. & 2 Jonth. shuttle mkrs
Cranmer Rev James Stuart, B.D. master of the Grammar School
3 Craven Wm. flock dir. & E. dress mkr
Firth J. cooper ‖ Brown J. sexton
Grant Rev Jph. B. B.A., incumbent of Oxenhope
Greenwood Wm. mfr. *Oxenhope Hs*
Hartley Wm. tinner & brazier, P.O.

Hudson John, painter, &c
Hughes Rev Geo. (Wes.) West lane
1 Lambert Robert, druggist
Lambert Thomas, plumber & glazier
Merall Edwin, mfr.; h *Ebor House*, and Hartley; h *Cook gate*
Murgatroyd John & Rd. corn millers
Nicholls Rev. A.B. curate
2 Ogden Jas. asst. overseer & regr
Parker Thomas, temperance hotel
Pickles Mr Michl. & John, toll colr
Redman Joseph, church clerk, &c
3 Taylor George, Esq. & Mrs Mary
Thomas James & Rd. P. wine and spirit merchants
Townend John, woolstapler
Wadsworth John, hairdresser
Whalley Mr J. ‖ 2 Whitehead Wm.
Wood Humphrey, painter & glazier
2 Wright Jonathan, Wm. & Lupton, spinners

INNS AND TAVERNS

2 Bay Horse, James Roberts
Black Bull, John Sugden
3 Cross Inn, Joseph Greenwood
Fleece, Hannah Stancliffe
3 Friendly Inn, Wm. Robinson
King's Arms, Wilson Greenwood
2 Lamb, John Horsfall
3 New Inn, Joshua Sunderland
2 New Inn, Robert Pickles
Shoulder of Mutton, Far Oxenhope
Sun, Robert Stoney, West lane
Waggoners' Inn, George Whitaker
White Lion, Joseph Sharp

ACADEMIES.

Smith John B.
Sumerscale Wm.
3 Sunderland A.

BEERHOUSES.

Greenwood J.
Marshall J.
Parker Wm.

BLACKSMITHS.

Gledhill Henry
Lund John
Moore Wm.
3 Scarborough J.
Whitaker James

98

BOOKSELLERS, &c.
Greenwood John
Leighton Archbd.

BOOT & SHOEMKS.
Akroyd Jonathan
2 Beaver John
3 Craven Joseph
1 Dawson Joseph
Hird Squire
Holt Joseph
Hudson Henry
Hudson Isaac
Hudson Isc. jun.
Newell Wm.
Roper Abraham
3 Scarborough Jns
Thornton Wm.
Taylor Joseph
3 Wilman Holmes
Whitham Wm.

BUTCHERS.
2 Feather James
Garnett Wm.
Greenwood Wilsn
Holmes John
Holmes Joseph
Moore John
2 Roberts James
3 Sharp J.
2 Stoney Thomas
2 Whitaker J.
3 Wignall John

CLOGGERS.
3 Craven Joseph
Fearnside Joseph
Hartley John
Helliwell Wm.
Mosley John
Murgatroyd Jph.
Sugden John

FARMERS.
2 Akroyd James
Bankroft Abm.
Binns John
1 Boocock C.
1 Brooksbank Wm.
Butterfield Abm.
Cousin James
Crabtree James
Dawson John
Dawson Joseph
Dean Joseph
3 Dugdale John
2 Dyson David
2 Foster Jonas
Garnett Wm.
3 Gott Joseph
Greenwood James
Halstead Wm.
Hartley Joseph
Hartley Wm.
Heaton Michael
Heaton Robert
Helliwell Thos.
3 Hey James
3 Holdsworth Jas.
Holdsworth Rt.
1 Hoyle Wm.
3 Hudson Eml.
Murgatroyd Rt.
Murgatroyd Ths.
1 Parker David
Pickles Michael
Ratcliff J.
1 Rushworth Wm.
3 Shackleton Benj.
3 Spencer Fredk.
Sunderland Jph.
Sutcliffe Holmes
Taylor George

Terry John
2 Whitaker Jtn.

GROCERS, &c.

Appleyard J.
2 Bankroft Timy.
Brown Robert
Brown Wm.
3 Craven John
Driver James
Firth Elizabeth
Firth Dnl. *draper*
3 Greenwood Jph
3 Greenwood Sus.
Greenwood John
Hartley (Hanb.) & Thomas (B.)
3 Hartley James
Hartley Betty
Hartley John
Hartley Timothy
Helliwell Betty
Hird John
Holmes Wm.
3 Hudson Emanl.
Hudson James
Hudson John
3 Hudson Saml.
Lambert John
Leighton Archbd.
Moore John
Newell John, *dpr*.
3 Redman John
Roper Wm.
3 Rushworth Ths.
Shackleton Jph.
Sugden Wm.
West Thomas
3 Whitaker John
Whitham Wm.
Wood Joseph

Wright Edward
Wright Grace
Wright Mary

JOINERS, &c.

are Cabt. Mks.;
& † Wheelwrights.
*Charnock Jas.
*Hartley James
*Murgatroyd Noh
*Roper James
3 Rushworth Geo.
†Sutcliffe John
*Wood Robert
*Wood Wm.
†Wright Pickles
*Wright Robert

PLASTERERS.

Greenwood John
Ingham Emanuel
Kendall John
Moore John

STONE MASONS.

Barstow David
Binns Wm.
Bottomley Thos.
2 Crabtree Wm.
Gregson James
2 Shackleton Wm.
3 Shackleton Wm.
Walmsley Wm.

SURGEONS.

Hall Edw. South
Ingham Amos

TAILORS.

Binns Benj.
Binns Wm.
Greenwood John
3 Holmes Jonas

2 Overend Isaac
Pickles Joseph O.
Redhough Joseph
Sugden Jonathan
Turner Wm.
Wood Greenwood

WORSTED SPINRS.
& MANFRS.

2 Akroyd John O.
Butterfield Bros.
Craven John and Joseph
2 Feather (John)
& Speck (John)
1 Greenwood Wm.
Hartley J. *Sutton*
Kershaw Brothers
Lambert James
Merrall Brothers, *Ebor Mill*
Mitchell James
2 Pickles Rt. & Co.
Sugden Jonas & Brothers
Thomas Wm. jun
2 Watson Robert
2 Wright J. & Bros

OMNIBUS
*To Bradford and
Halifax on market
days; and to meet
trains at Keighley*
Whitaker Jonth.

CARRIERS.
Hartley Robert
Pickles Michael
Todd Wm.
Whitham James

The *Yorkshire Directory*, 1848

3.7(c)   Haworth and the surrounding area

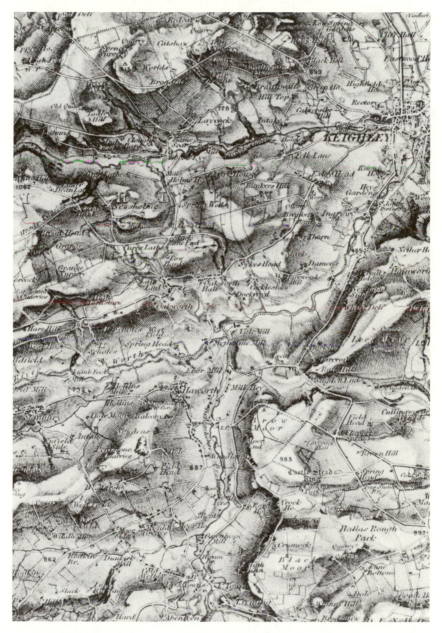

Ordnance Survey, England and Wales, one inch to one mile, reprint
1857

Questions

1   What different sorts of information can be obtained from directories? How can the historian use this information?
2   Why should the historian be cautious when using directories as evidence?
3   In what ways did the variety of occupations in Haworth change between 1823 and 1848 [3.7(a) and (b)]? Attempt an explanation of these changes.
4   In what ways is it possible to classify the occupations in Haworth?
5   What are the main differences between occupations in Haworth [3.7(a) and (b)] and Little Wratting in Suffolk [1.13(c)]?
6   The Industrial Revolution did not see the end of the rural industrial worker. How does the experience of Haworth demonstrate the validity of this statement?

The industrial experience is one that always requires skills, but the skills do not remain the same. The factories challenged the traditional structure of masters and apprentices. Skilled artisans experienced some dilution of their status by unskilled 'cheap-men'. Population increase, technological change and the vagaries of the trade cycle meant that competition for work increased. The gap between 'distress' and 'prosperity' was a narrow one.

4 The industrial experience – change as threat

In 1780 many handworkers were at the top of the wages league. By 1850 those who remained in hand trades were at its base. Why did this change occur and with what social consequences? Changes in technology, especially in textiles, led to an initial surge in demand for spinners and particularly handloom weavers. Mass production was achieved 'by dint of unremitting bodily effort'. But how valid was the notion of a 'golden age', what the poet Southey called 'contentment spinning at the cottage door'?

4.1 'The golden age of this great trade 1788 to 1803'

The old loom-shops being insufficient, every lumber-room, even old barns, cart-houses and out-buildings of any description, were repaired, windows broke through the old blank walls and all fitted up for loom-shops. This source of making room being at length exhausted, new weavers' cottages, with loom-shops, rose up in every   5
direction . . . both as cottagers and small farmers, even with three times their former rents, they might be truly said to be placed in a higher state of 'wealth, peace and godliness' by the great demand for, and high price of their labour than they had ever before experienced. Their dwellings and small gardens clean and neat – all the family   10
well clad – the men with each a watch in his pocket and the women dressed to their own fancy – the church crowded to excess every Sunday – every house well furnished with a clock in elegant mahogany or fancy case – handsome tea services in Staffordshire ware, with silver or plated sugar-tongs and spoons – Birmingham,   15
Potteries and Sheffield wares for necessary use and ornament, wherever a corner cupboard or shelf could be placed to shew them off – many cottage families had their cow, paying so much for the summer's grass, and about a statute acre of land laid out for them in some croft or corner, which they dressed up as a meadow for hay in   20
the winter.

William Radcliffe, *Origin of Power-Loom Weaving*, 1828, pp. 59–67

4.2   The 'golden age' illustrated

Hand-spinning, reeling with the clock-reel and boiling yarn

Linen manufacture – winding, warping and weaving

4.3   The handworkers comment!

Certainly we prefer having work in our own homes. We can begin
sooner or later and we do as we like in that respect, and those of us
who have families have an opportunity in one way or another of
training them up in some little business . . . Hand-loom work in the
weaver's own cottage gratifies that innate comfort and independence   5
which all more or less feel by leaving the workman entirely the
master of his own time and sole guide of his actions. He can play or
idle as feeling and inclination lead him; rise early or late and apply
himself as assiduously or carelessly as he pleases and work at any
time by increased exertions hours previously sacrificed to indulgence   10
or recreation. There is scarcely another condition of any of our
working population thus free of external authority.

**Report of the Select Committee appointed to Consider the State of
the Woollen Manufacture in England, 1806, vol. iii**

4.4   Wages in the cotton industry – weekly income of workers

Date	Weekly income	Date	Weekly income
1797	18s 9d	1805	23s 0d
1798	19s 9d	1806	20s 0d
1799	18s 6d	1807	17s 3d
1800	18s 9d	1808	13s 3d
1801	18s 6d	1809	14s 0d
1802	21s 0d	1810	14s 3d
1803	20s 0d	1811	12s 3d
1804	20s 0d	1812	14s 0d

*Amounts in shillings (s) and pence (d); 12d = 1s (5p), 20s = £1 (100p)

**G. H. Wood, *History of wages in the cotton trade during the past
hundred years*, 1910, p. 112**

Questions

1   In what ways do documents **4.1** and **4.2** show the notion of the
    'golden age' in the textile industry?
2   How do documents **4.2** and **4.4** support this view?
3   How convincing do you find the idea of the 'golden age' contained in
    this evidence [**4.1–4.4**]?

4   'Contentment spinning at the cottage door'; 'mass production by dint
         of unremitting bodily effort'. Explain the difference in emphasis of
         these two contemporary opinions.

But increasingly textile handworkers of all types were threatened by
changing technology and fashions. Their response was sometimes violent
to both property and persons. Document **4.5** examines the failure of riots in
Wiltshire:

4.5

         In July 1802 considerable riots and outrages took place in Wiltshire
and Somerset, in consequence of an attempt by some of the master
clothiers of those counties to set up a machine for dressing cloth
called a gig mill. This machine was from various causes obnoxious to
the workmen, and from an apprehension it is supposed of the   5
disturbances which the first introduction of it had never been set up
in the above counties, although it had been for many years in use in
Gloucestershire as well as other parts; it had even been by no means
unusual for the clothiers of Wiltshire and of some other districts
where it was not worked to send their cloths a distance to be dressed   10
by it. The disturbances above related were not quelled without
serious consequences, the discontents continuing from the workmen
learning that there was to be found in the statute book an ancient law
prohibiting under heavy penalties the use of a machine called a gig
mill (though doubts existed as to whether it was the machine which   15
now bore that denomination) and they conceived the project of
preventing its further establishment by calling the above statute into
operation.

**Report from the Select Committee appointed to Consider the State
of the Woollen Manufacture in England, 1806, vol. i**

Questions

1   In what ways were the riots caused by new technology [4.5]?
2   How had the clothiers in Wiltshire dealt with the problem of
         opposition to gig mills before 1802?
3   Why did the workers resurrect 'an ancient law' [4.5, line 13]?

These southern workers in combination with small clothiers in Yorkshire
decided to petition parliament to put the neglected statutes into force. This

alliance of workers and employers did lead to government considering the case with more care than if the workers had petitioned alone.

4.6   Government response

But your committee would be wanting to the important subject entrusted to their consideration if they were to forebear remarking that if the principles on which the use of these particular machines is objected to were once admitted it would be impossible to draw the line or to forsee the fateful extent of their application. No one will   5
deny that if parliament had acted on such principles fifty years ago the woollen manufacture would never have attained to half its present size. The rapid and prodigious increase of late years in the manufacture and commerce of this country is universally known as well as the effects of that increase by revenue and national strength;   10
and in considering the immediate cause of that augmentation it will appear that under the favour of providence it is principally to be ascribed to the general spirit of enterprise and industry among a free and enlightened people left to the unrestrained exercise of their talents in the employment of a vast capital; pushing to the utmost the   15
principle of the division of labour; calling on all the resources of scientific research and mechanical ingenuity; and finally availing themselves of all the benefits to be derived from visiting foreign countries.

Report from the Select Committee appointed to Consider the State of the Woollen Manufacture in England, 1806, vol. i

Questions

1   What arguments did the government use to justify their repeal of the old statutes [4.6].
2   How far is this extract [4.6] a statement of the virtues of 'free trade'?
3   Paternalism in decline. How valid an assertion is this of the woollen agitation from 1803–6?

The focal point of agitation then moved north. This was the result partially of the West Country workers abandoning their fight but also because of the increasing concentration of woollen production in Yorkshire. During the Luddite disturbances from 1810 to 1813 Yorkshire was one of the main centres of agitation. Luddism also existed in the Midlands, Lancashire and Cheshire, though for different reasons.

4.7   The framework knitters' declaration

BY THE FRAMEWORK KNITTERS
A DECLARATION

Whereas by the charter granted by our late sovereign Lord Charles
the Second by the Grace of God King of Great Britain France and
Ireland, the Framework Knitters are empowered to break and destroy 5
all Frames and Engines that fabricate articles in a fraudulent and
deceitful manner and destroy all Framework Knitters' Goods
whatsoever that are so made and whereas a number of deceitful
unprincipled and intriguing persons did attain an Act to be passed in
the Twenty Eighth Year of our present sovereign . . . whereby it was 10
enacted that persons entering by force into any House Shop or Place
to break or destroy Frames should be adjudged guilty of Felony as
we are fully convinced that such Act was obtained in the most
fraudulent interested and electioneering manner and that the
Honorable the Parliament of Great Britain was deceived as to the   15
motives and intentions of the persons who obtained such Act we
therefore the Framework Knitters do hereby declare the aforesaid Act
to be null and void to all intents and purposes . . . And whereas we
declare that the aforementioned Charter is as much in force as though
no such Act had been passed . . . And we do hereby declare to all   20
Hosiers Lace Manufacturers and Proprietors of Frames that we will
break and destroy all manner of Frames whatsoever that make the
following spurious articles and all Frames . . . that do not pay regular
prices heretofore agreed to the Masters and Workmen – All print net
Frames making single press and Frames not working by the rack and 25
rent and not paying the price regulated in 1810 – whereas all plain
silk Frames not making work according to the gage – Frames not
marking the work according to quality, whereas all Frames of
whatsoever description the workmen of whom are not paid in the
current coin of the realm will invariably be destroyed . . .   30
    Given under my hand this first day of January 1812.
God protect the Trade   Ned Lud's Office
                  Sherwood Forest

**The Declaration of the Framework Knitters, Home Office Papers,
42/119**

4.8 General Ludd's triumph – a song

The guilty may fear, but no vengeance he aims
At the honest man's life or estate
His wrath is entirely confined to wide frames
And to those that old princes abate.
These Engines of mischief were sentenced to die   5
By unanimous vote of the Trade;
And Ludd who can all opposition defy
Was the grand Executioner made.

And when in the work of destruction employed
He himself to no method confines   10
By fire and by water he gets them destroyed
For the Elements aid his designs.
Whether guarded by Soldiers along the Highway
Or closely secured in the room,
He shivers them up both by night and by day,   15
And nothing can soften their doom . . .

Let the wise and the great lend their aid and advice
Nor e'er their assistance withdraw
Till full fashioned work at old fashioned price
Is established by Custom and Law.   20
Then the Trade when this arduous contest is o'er
Shall raise in full splendour its head,
And colting* and cutting and squaring no more
Shall deprive honest workmen of bread.

*colting refers to employing more apprentices than allowed by local by-laws

Home Office 42/119, 27 January 1811, printed in full in J. L. Hammond and B. Hammond, *The Skilled Labourer*, Longman, 1979, p. 212

Questions

1   What are the main arguments employed in documents **4.7** and **4.8** to justify machine breaking?
2   How convincing do you find these arguments? Explain your reasons.
3   The framework knitters believed that they were upholding 'Custom and Law' [**4.8, line 20**]. How could they maintain this?

4   The framework knitters failed to understand that it was quantity not
quality that the employers wanted. Discuss.

The evidence for Luddism is often disordered and a more or less coherent
account of what happened has to be pieced together from the semi-literate
scribblings of Luddites themselves, or from 'intelligence', often obtained
from spies. These gave a picture of conspiracy or a 'general rising' which a
Select Committee of the House of Lords took very seriously.

4.9   Luddism in Lancashire

The discontent which had thus first appeared about Nottingham, and
had to some degree extended into Derbyshire and Leicestershire, had
before this period been communicated to other parts of the country
. . . in Cheshire, where anonymous letters were at the same time
circulated, threatening to destroy the machinery used in the   5
manufactures of that place, and in that and the following months
attempts were made to set on fire two different manufactories . . .
houses were plundered by persons in disguise, and a report was
industriously circulated that a general rising would take place on 1st
of May, or early in that month.   10
    The spirit of riot and disturbance was extended to many other
places, and particularly to Ashton-under-Lyne, Eccles and
Middleton; at the latter place the manufactory of Mr Burton was
attacked on the 20th of April, and although the rioters were then
repulsed, and five of their numbers were killed by the military force   15
assembled to protect the works, the second attack was made on the
22nd of April, and Mr Burton's dwelling house was burnt before
military assistance could be brought to his support; when troops
arrived to protect the works, they were fired upon before the rioters
could be dispersed, several of them were killed and wounded;   20
according to the accounts received, at least three were killed and
twenty wounded.
    On the 4th of April riots again prevailed at Stockport; the house of
Mr Goodwin was set on fire and his steam-looms were destroyed. In
the following night a meeting of rioters . . . was surprised and   25
dispersed; contributions were also levied in the neighbourhood, at the
houses of gentlemen and farmers . . . Nocturnal meetings for the
purpose of miltary exercise were frequent; arms were seized in
various places by the disaffected; the house of a farmer near

Manchester was plundered, and a labourer coming to his assistance   30
was shot.

The manner in which the disaffected have carried on their
proceedings, is represented as demonstrating an extraordinary degree
of concert, secrecy and organization. Their signals were well
contrived and well established, and any attempt to detect and lay   35
hold of the offenders was generally defeated.

**Report of the Select Committee of the House of Lords on the
Disturbed State of certain Counties, printed in Annual Register,
1812, pp. 386–8**

Questions

1   What caused discontent in these industrial areas?
2   How does document **4.9** build up the idea of a 'general rising'?
3   How far were spies acting as 'agents provocateurs' in Lancashire?

Two attempts were made to burn West Houghton steam-weaving factory
near Bolton. The first attempt on Thursday 9 April 1812 failed, and a
second was fixed for Sunday 19 April. But all that happened was a meeting
at Dean Moor.

4.10   Violence

'That on his arrival at the Meeting they were discoursing on the Act
of Queen Elizabeth which empowered the Magistrates to raise wages
to the price of Provisions, on the bad government of the Town
particularly the management of the Overseers, who kept the Poor
waiting twenty or thirty hours a week for their allowance.   5
    'That the Orders in Council and the Conduct if several
manufacturers were reprobated, the price of Provisions and the future
prosperity of Trade were discussed.
    'That on the arrival of the Blacks or Persons with their Faces
blackened, the whole were formed in a Circle and one of the Blacks   10
addressed the Meeting, asking what was to be done, recommending
good Order, wishing all to speak freely but only one at a time. When
he ended, a Man with a clean Face began a speech describing the
Situation of the Country, the Hardships and Miseries of the
industrious Weavers and Mechanics, which he attributed to the War,   15
the Orders in Council were reprobated, and also the System of
reducing Wages instead of diminishing the quantity of work in a

given time, he recommended likewise a Subscription to apply to Lord
Ellenborough for a Mandamus to compel the Magistrates to do their
duty.   20

'That he was answered by one who was disfigured who said that it
was all damned Nonsense to talk of Law as no Justice would be done
except they did it themselves, that they had lost time and spent
Money to no purpose, he noticed the Proceedings at Nottingham,
Yorkshire, Stockport and Middleton and hoped they would do their   25
part which was to burn the Weaving Factory at West Houghton but
this was rejected by all but the Blacks.

'That the Majority wishing to go home they were told the Military
and the Constables were on the roads, and that it was impossible to
get to Bolton without being arrested.   30

'That they were also told there were 200 Men waiting at Chowbent
wishing to be joined by Bolton, and if they went to Chowbent by the
time they got back the Military would be dismissed. That it was
agreed to go, and being cold with standing so long on the Moor, he
walked pretty sharp on passing the Four Lane Ends in Hulton there   35
were only three in his Company.

'That he met only three drunken Men, that he stopped at the
Bridge near Chowbent till the rest came up which was more than half
an hour.

'That they then proceeded to the Cross where a Pistol was fired,   40
three Cheers given and then they were ordered to disperse.'

**The deposition of John Heys, from Home Office Papers 42/128,
printed in full in J. L. Hammond and B. Hammond, *The Skilled
Labourer*, Longman, 1979, pp. 230–1**

Questions

1   What are the main points of criticism made at Dean Moor [4.10]?
2   What picture of Luddite organisation emerges from this document?
3   Luddism in Lancashire – a plea for justice. Discuss.

4.11   Luddism in Yorkshire – a letter to a Huddersfield Master in 1812

SIR,
        Information has just been given in, that you are a holder of
those detestable Shearing Frames, and I was desired by my men to

write to you, and give you fair warning to pull them down, and for
that purpose I desire that you will understand I am now writing to   5
you, you will take notice that if they are not taken down by the end
of next week, I shall detach one of my lieutenants with at least 300
men to destroy them, and further more take notice that if you give us
the trouble of coming thus far, we will increase your misfortunes by
burning your buildings down to ashes, and if you have the   10
impudence to fire at any of my men, they have orders to murder you
and burn all your Housing . . . and as the views of intentions of me
and my men have been so misrepresented, I will take this
opportunity of stating them . . . the Government and the Public
know that the grievances of such a number of men is not to be made   15
sport of, for by the last returns there were 2782 sworn Heroes bound
in a Bond of necessity, either to redress their grievances or perish in
the attempt, in the army of Huddersfield alone, nearly double sworn
men in Leeds, by the latest Letters from our Correspondents, we
learn that the Manufacturers of the following places are going to rise   20
and join us in redressing their wrongs viz Manchester, Wakefield,
Halifax, Bradford, Sheffield, Oldham, Rochdale and all the Cotton
Country . . . the weavers of Glasgow and many Parts of Scotland will
join us, the papists in Ireland are rising to a Man, so that they are
likely to find the soldiers something else to do than idle in   25
Huddersfield . . . we hope for assistance from the French Emperor in
shaking off the Yoke of the Rottenest, wickedest and most Tyrannical
Government that ever existed, then down comes the Hanover
Tyrants and all our tyrants from the greatest to the smallest, and we
will be governed by a just Republic, and may the Almighty hasten   30
those happy times is the wish and prayer of Millions in this Land,
but we won't only pray but we will fight, the Red Coats shall know
when the proper time's come, we will never lay down our arms till
the House of Commons passes an act to put down all the machinery
hurtfull to the Commonality and repeal that to the Frame Breakers –   35
but we petition no more, that won't do, fighting must,
Signed by the General of the Army of Redressers
NED LUDD
Clerk

Home Office Papers 40/41, printed in full in G. D. H. Cole and A. W.
Filson, *British Working Class Movements*, 1951, pp. 114–15

Questions

1   What were the causes of Luddism in Yorkshire according to document **4.11**?
2   What information can be obtained from document **4.11** on the organisation of Luddism? How much of an overestimate was it?
3   Economic grievances necessitated revolutionary change. Discuss this statement in relation to document **4.11**.
4   Using documents **4.7** to **4.11**, account for the differences between the Luddism of Lancashire, Yorkshire and the Midlands.

The response of the authorities to Luddism was harsh. Large numbers of troops were deployed in the North and Midlands under General Maitland. This caused a great deal of annoyance to peaceful inhabitants upon whom they were billeted. A network of spies largely supplied by Joseph Nadin of Manchester was introduced. Penalties for giving and taking illegal oaths were increased from July 1812 and machine-breaking became a capital offence a year later. By contrast a strike by Scottish cotton weavers in 1812, according to a letter written to the Home Secretary, 'seemed particularly cautious to avoid Luddism'. Though there were further outbreaks of machine-breaking until the 1830s, physical and largely unorganised action ceased to play a major part in attempts by woollen and cotton workers to improve their conditions.

In 1818 wage reductions led to strikes by four groups. First the Stockport jenny spinners went on strike and after six weeks the employers agreed to some increase in wages. In June the power loom weavers followed suit but action under the Combination Act by employers led to troops forcing them back to work in August without any increase in wages. Bricksetters, joiners, carpenters and dyers achieved wage increase by strike action. Finally the Manchester cotton spinners began their agitation.

4.12   Prosperity?

No class of people have had such constant and uniform employment for the last twenty-eight years, as they have had : and this advantage the spinner enjoys at the risk and expense of his employer.

Manchester Chronicle, 15 August 1818

4.13   Cotton spinners, 1818 – statement 1

To the Inhabitants of Manchester and its Vicinity . . . We the
distressed Journeymen Cotton Spinners have been working a
considerable Time for Prices very inadequate to procure even the
coarsest necessaries of Life for ourselves and Families, and have been
obliged by degrees to part with our Goods and Clothing, and are now   5
unable to pay the demands which Justice requires from us; but
having solicited our Employers for an advance of Prices (which has
been refused) yet from the present State of the Market, we have
every Reason to conclude that our reasonable Request ought to have
been complied with, and their Profits (had their humanity kept Pace   10
with their Avarice) would still have enabled them to live in affluence.

Home Office Papers 42/178

4.14   Cotton spinners, 1818 – statement 2

We are stated in all the papers to have turned out for an advance of
wages; this we admit to be in part true, but not absolutely so. Two
years ago, when our employers demanded a reduction of ten hanks,
they affirmed that the state of the market imperiously called for such
reduction; but when the market would admit of an advance, they   5
would willingly give it. We depended on their honour, and continued
to labour for more than 12 months at the reduction proposed. About
10 months since, on comparing the price of cotton and yarn, we
found that the markets would allow our employers to fulfil their
promise; we therefore solicited them to that purpose, and only wished 10
to be reinstated in the same prices we worked at previously to that
reduction . . . It is asserted that our average wages amount to 30s or
40s per week – it is evident that this statement was made by some
individual either ignorant or interested. In 1816, the average clear
wages of the spinners in Manchester was about 24s, they were then   15
reduced from 20 to 25 per cent, and have ever since laboured under
that reduction. And it is remarked, that spinners relieve their own
sick, as well as subcribe to other casualties; therefore, when their
hours of labour, which are from 5 in the morning until 7 in the
evening (and in some mills longer) of unremitting toil, in rooms   20
heated from 70 to 90 degrees, are taken into consideration, we believe

the public will say with us, that no body of workmen receive so
inadequate a compensation for their labour.

**Annual Register, 1818, Chronicle pp. 10–11, printed in full in J. L.
Hammond and B. Hammond, *The Skilled Labourer*, Longman, 1979,
pp. 79–80**

4.15   Discrepancy explained?

Our Master keeps a Book and takes off 6*d* the 1*s* for Big Wheels and
4*d* the 1*s* for little wheels and I have gone home with 12*s* and
sometimes 10*s* a week. It is a false statement of him (that we were
getting 30*s* a week) and he said he could bring his Books before the
Magistrates and shew that we got 35*s* a week.

**Examination of John Hague, 29 August 1818, Home Office Papers 42/
179**

Questions

1   What are the main arguments employed by the cotton spinners [4.13
      and 4.14]?
2   How can the differences between the employers' and workers' cases
      be explained [4.12–4.15]?

4.16   Appeal for help

SIR,
       The Spinners of Manchester have authorized me to solicit you to
join in their union of trade, as all trades in England are uniting in
one body for Trade and Reform, and you are desired to send a
delegate to all Meetings to consult matters over and to inform you   5
that you will be supported in your Trade in turn; A letter was
received from London this day from the Silk Weavers wishing to join
them and offering their support, they have taken all the big pieces in
pay lest they should do mischief and their number is 800, they have
no less now in pay than 3,000 in the whole, we must try our Friends   10
in every corner of the Land wherever they can be found and which
every exertion is now making to accomplish and hope it will
contribute to carry them into ultimate success is now making to seem
quite determined not to return to their Egyptian Slavery and haughty

language and cruel usage for the same terms they quitted it for, and   15
indeed nothing less than a serious determination will ever bring their
employers to any reason for if Manchester is obliged to give way at
least the Work People in this and every other Town may bid an
everlasting farewell to having any comfort or above one half of the
Wages that will supply the common necessaries of life.   20

I am for the Staley Bridge Spinners and by their Order,
Gentlemen, Your obedient Servant,

JAMES FIELDING

To all Colliers in
Newton Duckenfield Hyde and Staley Bridge

An intercepted letter dated 7 August 1818, Home Office Papers 42/179

Questions

1   What information can you obtain from this letter [4.16] on the
position of the spinners after five weeks on strike?
2   Why was support from other workers sporadic in extent?
3   Why did a 'general trades union' not succeed in the period between
1800 and 1850?

The spinners were utterly defeated. The fourth group to act were the
weavers who were struggling to escape from a standard of living marked
by poverty and degradation.

4.17 'The Poor Weavers'

We the Weavers of this Town and Neighbourhood respectively
request your attention to the wretched situation to which we have a
long time been exposed, owing to the extreme depression of our
Wages, and request you to call a Meeting amongst yourselves, and try
if there cannot be some alleviation made to our Sufferings, by an   5
advance thereof, as you well know they are not adequate to purchase
the common Necessaries of Life. We are of opinion that if you would
exert yourselves as a body, the thing might be accomplished without
affecting your profits, which we are far from wishing to injure.

**Address to the manufacturers of Oldham, 15 July 1818, Home Office
Papers 42/178**

4.18   The Bury meeting, 27 July 1818

GENTLEMEN. It is the gulph that absorbs all the faculties of body
and mind we address you, supposing you capable of ameliorating the
sufferings of an immense body of useful Artizans . . . we hope your
minds are not become so callous, not yet so indifferent to our
situation, as to rejoice over our misfortunes, thereby increasing your   5
triumph in proportion to our calamity, or suffer a degree of
unconcern to our case . . . we ask you for an advance of seven
shillings on the pound, in this you must admit we have confined
ourselves within the boundaries of moderation, as several other
branches of the trade have called for a greater advance than the whole   10
of our income, but we trust you will not look on us with contumacy,
on account of our pacific dispositions, proved by our moderate
demand.

**Address to the cotton manufacturers of Lancashire, Yorkshire,
Cheshire etc., Home Office Papers 42/178, printed in full in J. L.
Hammond and B. Hammond, *The Skilled Labourer*, Longman, 1979,
pp. 88–9**

Questions

1   What are the main complaints of the weavers [4.17 and 4.18]?
2   What arguments do the weavers use to justify their demands for
      better wages [4.17 and 4.18]?
3   The weavers were generally 'non-political' in their approach. What
      does this mean and how do documents **4.17** and **4.18** demonstrate
      this approach?

The weavers were law-abiding, unlike the spinners, and confined their
action to processions and meetings during the strike. But the prosecution
and imprisonment of their leaders ended the strike without their objective
of minimum wages being achieved. Interestingly, after 1819 employers
too began to demand minimum wages – a response to falling demand.

But was decline just seen in terms of the threat of technological
innovation?

4.19   William Jackson to the Home Secretary, 1817

a statement of matters of fact, and things as they really are in this
Town [Leicester] and Neighbourhood. The frame-Work Knitters in
consequence of the reduction of their Wages are reduced to the
lowest state of misery and wretchedness, and if the present system of
giving low wages is persisted in, the whole of the common people   5
must soon become paupers. One cause of this state of things is the
Combination Acts, which is unjust in its principles, and impolitic in
its application. If this Act had never been enforced mechanics would
be in a great measure . . . enabled to resist their employers in
reducing their Wages . . . All ranks of People in this Town see and   10
feel the evil of the present system of giving low Wages . . . It is not
the want of employment of which we complain but the lowness of
our Wages, the hands out of work being comparatively few. You have
legislated to keep up the price of Corn, and it is but just that you
should legislate to keep up the price of labour.

Home Office Papers 42/160, printed in full in J. L. Hammond and B.
Hammond, *The Skilled Labourer*, Longman, 1979, p. 197

4.20   Cultural deprivation

Their sole connection with the great community around them is their
weekly resort to the master's warehouse, which is assuredly no
powerful means of civilisation; and beyond this they are almost
alienated from all society. The influences which reach them are those
only of a religious character; and the feebleness of these has already   5
been shown*. The great body of the weaving and framework knitting
populations are similarly dispersed; and the absenteeism of so many
of the employers, except agents who are not real capitalists, will, I
doubt not, be found everywhere to have a great, though not always
an obvious, effect on the condition of the labouring people . . .   10
through the want of the moral bonds which should attach them to
society at large.

*the report placed great emphasis on the educational facilities available to the
Coventry weavers.

Joseph Fletcher, secretary to the Royal Commission on Handloom
Weavers in Parliamentary Papers, 1840, vol. xxiv, p. 205

4.21   Agricultural workers as threat, 1838

When there is a great demand for goods, the men who have been
working at less difficult fabrics are set to do the finer goods; and for
the lower and coarser fabrics, men and women from any other
employment can be put to the loom, and soon manage to do their
work passably well. Hence it is that at times when there is a great   5
demand for goods, if agricultural labourers be unemployed there is a
great influx into the weaver's trade in the villages of Norfolk by
persons of whom the regular weavers of Norwich made great
complaints.

Parliamentary Papers, 1840, vol. xxiii, p. 156

4.22   Machines should not be abused

Our machinery has hitherto been applied . . . to the raising and
gathering together of large heaps of wealth to the 'great' owners of it,
and to driving from the workshop the man who had to 'earn his
bread by the sweat of his brow' and dragging into his place . . . the
woman and child, inflicting upon them LONGER HOURS of toil   5
than the man had to endure before his suppression . . . Tell us not
that these things must continue . . . A better and more just
distribution of the fruits of toil must be made . . . That which is
itself one of the greatest of blessings must not continue to be made
into the greatest of scurges and curses. IT MUST BE   10
REGULATED! It must be used within due limits; and its benefits
must be diffused amongst and secured to all concerned.

***The Northern Star*, 5 February 1842**

Questions

1   How can documents **4.19** to **4.22** be used to argue that declining
      living standards were *not* just the result of new technology?
2   Were the results of introducing machines merely material or did they
      lead to cultural deprivation?
3   How effective is *The Northern Star* [**4.22**] in arguing that it was not
      machines but their abuse that led to deprivation?

Though the plight of cotton and woollen workers made the greatest impression later, in Chartism, there were many other handworkers whose conditions were equally affected – for example in clothing, lace, boot and shoe, nail and chain production. Outworkers and their employers were caught in the vice of economic advance and changing fashions. To remain competitive employers had to lower wages or introduce labour-saving machines to reduce costs. Distress led to workers' demands for justice whereas employers used the law to counter these demands. Economic reality shattered the notion of mutual and moral responsibility of employer and worker. Protective legislation was either ignored or repealed. Concern expressed in the various parliamentary enquiries was not turned into remedial action. Handworkers continued largely unprotected for the rest of the century – their attitudes often pre-industrial in form; their living standards declining; their social status decaying in a mechanised and profit-conscious society.

5 Reform – change or continuity? – the case of the poor

Population growth, urban expansion, economic depression on arable land, rising poor rates all combined to put pressure upon a changing society. The Elizabethan or 'old' poor law, even with its modifications and the widespread introduction of 'allowances on wages' – the so-called 'Speenhamland system' – was incapable of dealing effectively with the *scale* of the problem of the poor. The result was the 1834 Poor Law (Amendment) Act following a Royal Commission set up two years earlier. This led to the 'new' Poor Law. But how fundamental were the changes in this new law?

5.1 The Speenhamland system

When the Gallon Loaf of Second Flour, weighing 8lb 11 ozs shall cost 1/–.* Then every poor and industrious man shall have for his own support 3/– weekly, either produced by his own or his family's labour, or an allowance from the poor rates, and for the support of his wife and every other of his family 1/6.   5

When the Gallon Loaf shall cost 1/4. Then every poor and industrious man shall have 4/– weekly for his own and 1/10 for the support of every other of his family.

And so in proportion, as the price of bread rise or falls (that is to say) 3*d* to the man, and 1*d* to every other of the family, on every 1*d*   10 which the loaf rise above 1/–.

*Amounts are in shillings and pence (*s*/*d*); 12*d* = 1*s* (5p), 20*s* = £1 (100p).

Reading Mercury, 11 May 1795

5.2 Relief outside the workhouse

(a) County populations

County	Population in 1801 (in thousands)	Population in 1811 (in thousands)
Sussex	159	190
Berkshire	111	120
Wiltshire	184	192
Oxford	112	120

(b) Wheat prices per quarter*

1802	69s 10d
1812	126s 6d
1813	109s 9d
1814	74s 4d

*Amounts in shillings (s) and pence (d);
12d = 1s (5p), 20s = £1 (100p)

(c) Adults on permanent relief out of the workhouse

County	1802–3	1812–13	1813–14	1814–15
Sussex	9415	14472	14009	13058
Berkshire	5620	9453	9074	7175
Wiltshire	12500	16009	15144	13355
Oxford	6539	7792	7635	7134

**Printed in E. M. Tucker, *Britain 1760–1914*, Edward Arnold, 1977,
p. 35**

5.3 Rising cost of poor relief

Years	Sum levied	Sums expended on Relief (£)	Total expended (£)
1812–13	8 640 842	6 656 105	8 865 838
1813–14	8 388 974	6 294 584	8 511 863
1814–15	7 457 676	5 418 845	7 508 853
1815–16	6 937 425	5 724 506	***
1816–17	8 128 418	6 918 217	***
1817–18	9 320 440	7 890 148	***
1818–19	8 932 185	7 531 650	***
1819–20	8 719 655	7 329 594	8 672 252

*** for this period there is no account of the sums expended

**Based on Select Committee on Poor Rate Returns, Report V,
Appendix A, 1822**

5.4 Increase in poor rates

The great increase in the amount of the poor-rates of late years, I
conceive to be principally attributable to the lamentable degeneracy of

the labouring classes, and to the utter want of that spirit of independence of others, and reliance upon his own exertions for his support, which formerly characterised an English peasantry. There are few persons to be found, amongst the labouring classes, who will struggle to maintain their families without parochial assistance. The object with them is to get as much as possible from the parish; and a man whose average earnings during the year are fully sufficient to support his family, is frequently the person who receives the most in the shape of relief from the parish.

From Henry Everett, who covered parts of East Anglia for the Royal Commission, in Report from the Commissioners on the Poor Laws, 1834, Appendix A, Part 1, p. 682A

5.5   Criticism of allowances on wages

If men are induced to marry from the prospect of parish provision, with little or no chance of maintaining their families in independence, they are not only unjustly tempted to bring unhappiness and dependence upon themselves and their children, but are tempted, without knowing it, to injure all in the same class with themselves. A labourer who marries without being able to support a family may in some respects be considered as an enemy to all his fellow-labourers.

T. R. Malthus, *On Population*, ed. G. Himmelfarb, New York Modern Library, 1960, pp. 33–4

Questions

1   How did relief outside the workhouse increase after 1800 and what impact did this have on the poor rates [**5.2 and 5.3**]?

2   In what ways does the criticism of allowances on wages in documents **5.4** and **5.5** differ? Account for these differences.

3   Why were the 'dependent' poor an enemy to the rest of the poor according to Malthus [**5.5**]? Is his conclusion valid?

4   Was criticism of the 'Speenhamland system' in the early nineteenth century fair? In your answer discuss the work of historian Mark Blaug.

5   The rulers of society were abdicating their responsibility for the poor. Discuss.

6   Why did so many people regard poverty as a crime?

But was poverty a crime? To the paternalist, poverty was as it had always been, not a crime but a natural condition to be alleviated by those who were happily able to afford to. Relief testified to an obligation by society to care for the less fortunate who were unable to care for themselves.

5.6 Paternalism in action

A pauper named Sutton returned to the parish with his wife and child, having been away for some time and applied for relief and clothes for himself and his family. The overseers, suspecting that he possessed clothes, managed to get him and his wife out of the room, keeping the little girl in, and then asked the girl where her Sunday frock was. She answered that it was locked up in a box in Cambridge with other things. Here the mother came in to call the girl out, but the overseers would not let her go, whereupon the father [Sutton] came in with a bludgeon, and seized the child by the arm. The overseers held her, but her father pulling her so as to hurt her, they let her go and he took her out and beat her violently. He then returned, demanding relief, which they refused. He abused them dreadfully, threatening to rip one up, burn the town etc., and behaved with such violence that they were compelled to have him handcuffed and his legs tied and he was wheeled in a barrow to the magistrate, where they charged him with assault. The magistrate asked whether they could swear they were in bodily fear of Sutton, and they replying they were not, he dismissed the charge and ordered relief.

Printed in W.E.A., *In and Out of the Workhouse*, EARO 1978, pp. 3–4

5.7 Power to the landowners

By following the dictates of their own interests, landowners and farmers become, in the natural order of things, the best trustees and guardians for the public; when that order of things is destroyed, and a compulsory maintenance established for all who require it, the consequence cannot fail in the end to be equally ruinous to both parties.

Report of the Select Committee on the Poor Laws (1817), in Sessional Papers (Commons), 1819, vol. ii, p. 296

5.8   Seasonality of employment

For a certain period of the year at least . . . there is for the whole
county a surplus labouring population; as to the average degree of
surplus (per parish) or the average extent of the period, it is
impossible even to conjecture . . . the former varying from one to two
hundred men, the latter from one week to eleven months, in different   5
places.

Again, during another portion of the year, and this perhaps the
greater portion, there is undoubtedly no surplus labour, the surface of
the county sufficing at this period for the employment of the whole, if
fairly distributed.   10

Thirdly, during another very small portion of the year, namely one
month of harvest, there is actually a deficiency; for, beside the labour
on the spot, a great quantity of Irishmen, and labourers from the
southern counties, are employed with advantage.

**Report of Alfred Power, Report from the Commissioners on the Poor
Laws, Appendix A, Part 1, pp. 246A–9A**

5.9   Right to (wild) oats!

Of our Political Economy the following is a literal specimen – the
Speaker a Farmer a tenant of my own a rate payer, and therefore with
a right to voting in the Vestry – 'Poor folk have as much right to
bread as the rich, and that they can never have, till every man has
land enif to keep a coo – How is a poor man, let me ax, to have a wife 5
and eight children on his wage?' 'But why,' I ventured to suggest,
'Do men marry and get eight children without any likely means of
keeping them?' 'Why do folks marry!! thou maught as well ax why
they catch smallpox or ought like that – what wouldst thou do I
would like to know if left alone with that ere lass?' . . . it was   10
impossible to particularize what I would not do – so my friend
triumphantly continued – 'Nay, sir, that's a matter of God's own
ordering and man can't mind it – his very first command was
"Increase and multiply," and there's no going agin it.'

**R. W. Pilkington to Edwin Chadwick, 24 October 1834, Chadwick
Papers, University College Library, London**

Questions

1   Why did the magistrate overturn the decision of the overseers [5.6]?
    Was he justified in the decision? How do you account for it?
2   The debate was not really about the poor but power over the poor.
    How is this borne out in document **5.7**? Why were landowners
    concerned with their loss of power?
3   In what ways do documents **5.8** and **5.9** demonstrate a paternalistic
    attitude to the poor?
4   Using all four documents construct the paternalistic case for the
    rights of the poor.
5   Paternalism was a creed that spoke of 'rights' and 'obligations'.
    Political economy had little room for these. As a result Gertrude
    Himmelfarb can state that 'Poor relief was not a right, because the
    marketplace recognised neither rights nor obligations but only . . .
    "contracts" . . . freely entered into by free men . . . In that
    contractual world the pauper had no place.' Discuss and debate.

But why had poverty increased and what caused it? Alexis de Tocqueville
and Henry Mayhew provide two possible answers.[1]

5.10   Alexis de Tocqueville in 1833

In a country where the majority is ill-clothed, ill-housed, ill-fed, who
thinks of giving clean cloths, healthy foods, comfortable quarters to
the poor? The majority of the English, having all these things, regard
their absence as a frightful misfortune; society believes itself bound to
come to the aid of those who lack them, and cures evils which are not   5
even recognised elsewhere. In England, the average standard of living
man can hope for in the course of his life is higher than in any other
country in the world. This greatly facilitates the extension of
pauperism in the kingdom . . . But I am deeply convinced that any
permanent, regular, administration system whose aim will be to   10
provide for the needs of the poor, will breed more miseries than it can
cure, will deprave the population that it wants to help and comfort,
will in time reduce the rich to being no more than the tenant-farmers
of the poor, will dry up the sources of savings, will stop the
accumulation of capital, will retard the development of trade, will   15
benumb human industry and activity, and will culminate by

bringing about a violent revolution in the State, when the number of those who receive alms will have become as large as those who give it.

'Memoir on Pauperism' (1835), printed in Seymour Drescher (ed.), *De Tocqueville and Beaumont on Social Reform*, Harper and Row, 1968, pp. 10, 24–5

Questions

1   How does de Tocqueville distinguish between poverty and pauperism [5.10]? What arguments does he use to explain the growth of pauperism?
2   Why does de Tocqueville argue that the present Poor Law system was disastrous?
3   The 'Swing' riots of 1830 showed the inadequacy of the existing system of poor relief. Discuss.

5.11   Henry Mayhew in 1849

I purposed considering the whole of the metropolitan poor under three distinct phases – according as they will work, as they can't work and as they won't work. The causes of poverty among such as are willing to work appeared to me to be two: 1. The workman might receive for his labour less than sufficiency to satisfy his wants. 2. He might receive a sufficiency, and yet be in want, either from having to pay an exhorbitant price for the commodities he requires in exchange for his wages, or else from a deficiency of economy and prudence in the regulation of his desires by his means and chances of subsistence.

Henry Mayhew in *The Morning Chronicle*, printed in E. P. Thompson and E. Yeo (eds.), *The Unknown Mayhew*, Penguin, 1973, p. 122

Questions

1   What distinction did Henry Mayhew make between the metropolitan poor [5.11]?
2   What were the causes of poverty among those willing to work? How do these causes compare with those in rural areas?
3   The causes and types of poverty which Mayhew identified applied to all areas of British society in the first half of the nineteenth century. Discuss.

The Report of the Royal Commission, published in February 1834, condemned as both morally and economically disastrous a system which relieved mere poverty rather than absolute destitution. It concluded that 'the great source of abuse is outdoor relief afforded to the able-bodied'. Modern historians, notably Mark Blaug, have criticised its authors for selecting evidence which showed pre-determined conclusions. This was to weaken seriously the policies adopted after 1834.[2]

5.12   Revd Buller, vice-chairman of the Linton Guardians in Cambridgeshire

> Our progress upon the whole, as to the reduction of able-bodied pauperism, is most satisfactory. The new law did not come into operation with us till 29 August last [1835] and we have now scarcely a single application from persons of that description . . . The same idle and disreputable characters, the refuse of their respective   5 parishes, make their occasional appearances at the Board; but they meet with constant discouragement, and the workhouse is never accepted by them but as the very last resource . . . With respect to the behaviour of the poor, the farmers in general bear testimony to their improvement in civility to their employers, their greater care to   10 keep their places, and their endeavours to get their children into service.

From W.E.A. *In and Out of the Workhouse*, EARO 1978, pp. 34–5

5.13   Earl of Hardwicke, chairman of the Caxton-and-Arrington Union, Cambridgeshire

> We put up a hand corn-mill during the last winter, which employed 17 or 18 able-bodied men for a short time, but it was difficult to find hands to keep it at work. With regard to the condition of the labouring classes, I should say that a visible alteration has taken place in their manners; all farmers that I have conversed with say that they   5 are more respectful and civil in their behaviour and more regular to their time of work. The parishes of this Union have never been so free from crime. The cases brought before the magistrates at the petty sessions are much reduced. In the parish of Gamlingay the saving has been enormous and the able-bodied were during the winter employed   10 generally, never having above from 17 to 20 men out of work at any

one time: whereas the previous winters . . . have seen 100 men, on an
average, receiving parochial relief . . . I have no doubt that by a
steady and just administration of the law taking each case on its
merits, we shall next year be able to give you a report that will show a   15
greater saving, together with a large improvement in the moral state
of the community.

**Second Annual Report of the Poor Law Commissioners, Appendix B,
pp. 233–5**

Questions

1   What is meant by 'correct social attitudes'? Why were these
     important in the 1830s?
2   In what ways do documents **5.12** and **5.13** show some restoration of
     'correct social attitudes'? How does this demonstrate paternalist
     attitudes?
3   Historian Anthony Brundage argues that the 1834 Act marked a
     culmination of centuries of shaping the poor laws to the needs of
     landowners. How do documents **5.12** and **5.13** support this view?
4   Is Anthony Brundage right? Justify your answer.

But there was opposition to the new law.[3] This was widespread in
southern England between 1835 and 1837 where workhouses and
relieving officers were widely attacked.[4] In June 1836 a relieving officer in
the Henstead Union (Norfolk) received thirty stab wounds and a battering
to the head and face. In 1837 a mob gathered at Gainsborough station to
throw the officer into the River Trent only to find that he had got off the
train at the previous station.

5.14   The 'voice of the poor'

The petitioners, knowing that the farmers have not had the means of
paying them if they employed them, have endured many hardships
and privations without a murmur, but a most cruel, unnatural and
unfeeling power has sprung up with the New Poor Law, which has
the effect of lowering the wages of labourers and is in fact grinding   5
them down to the dust. The petitioners say that when out of
employment (as they frequently are a long time together) they can get
but a very short allowance of bread, no means of paying rent or
buying meat, drink or clothing, and must soon therefore be naked

and houseless; and after labouring to provide food for all other classes 10
to enjoy, they consider it unfair, unjust and cruel in the extreme for
them to be half famished in the midst of plenty. They are dismayed
and disgusted beyond anything they can describe, with the idea of
being shut up in one part of a prison and their wives and children in
separate parts because they are poor by no fault or act of their own, 15
under the false and deceitful pretence of bettering their conditions.
They therefore humbly and respectfully, but firmly and earnestly
pray, entreat and implore the house to protect them against such
oppression, and they hope the house will consider it one of its first
duties to provide such means as will bring fair prices and full 20
employment at fair wages, by which they may earn their livings as
they used to, by honest industry according to the station of life they
are placed in, and that the house will forthwith repeal this unfeeling
and un-English New Poor Law.

**Petition to Parliament by the labourers of Bourn, probably worded
by Revd F. H. Maberley, *Cambridge Chronicle*, 18 February 1837**

5.15(a) Ampthill Riots May 1835

To the Earl De Grey, St. James' Square
Magistrates Bench, Ampthill May 14th 1835

My Lord,
            In the close of our letter to your Lordship yesterday, we
promised to give your Lordship the earliest information of the 5
necessity of further aid, should such aid unfortunately be found
indispensable to repress the hostile spirit which has manifested itself
against the operation of the Poor Law Amendment Act. We greatly
regret that we are now compelled to acquaint your Lordship that a
very serious riot has this day occurred at Ampthill, which renders it 10
necessary for us, as Magistrates, to seek for some further power
beyond the means of enforcing the execution of the law now att our
disposal. A Body of about five hundred people assembled before the
Ampthill Workhouse while the Board of Guardians for the Union
were in delibration. They were in a state of great excitement, and 15
behaved with great violence. They used very violent language, broke
the windows of the Workhouse and assaulted the Guardians. Their
conduct became so violent and formidable as to render it necessary to

read the riot Act. This was done, and great numbers of the Mob still
remain undispersed . . .   20

My Lord,
        A body of twenty Policemen (Inspector Sandrock, 2
sergeants and 18 men) arrived at Ampthill about 10 o'clock this
Morning, by the aid of whom, in conjunction with the Special
Constables (96 initially and then a further 150) we have sworn into   25
office, we have been able to execute warrants against such of the
rioters as could be found, and some of them have been examined, and
are about to be committed to gaol.
        There has been no farther rioting today, and we trust we shall
be able to preserve the public peace with the force now at our   30
command . . .
        We have the honour to be, My lord, your Lordship's Obedient
Servants, Thomas Barber, George Cardale, George Musgrave, Henry
Musgrave, James Beard.

Bedfordshire Record Office LCG12

5.15(b)

Present: Rev. George Cardale, Rev. Thomas Barber, Rev. James
Beard, George Musgrave and Henry M. Musgrave esquires.
Very few of the persons in Ampthill appointed special constables
having attended, summonses were made out for each, requiring
attendance forthwith, and delivered by the high constables. 96   5
persons from several parishes in the union took the oath as special
constables in the course of the day; and in the evening the bailiff of
Joseph Morris esquire and 39 of his labourers attended and took the
oath. The constables of Lidlington reported that they had proceeded,
with the assistance of the constables of Ampthill, to execute the   10
warrant for the apprehension of the persons at Lidlington, but that
they had given them up as a consequence of the threats of a large
mob in Millbrook. The magistrates, on the application of the
members of the board of guardians had met and explained to the
persons then assembling at the house of industry of the mistake   15
under which they laboured as to the operation of the poor law act.
        The guardians returned about 1.30 and reported that their
endeavours had been fruitless; that the windows of the house of

industry were all broken in; and they had been personally attacked by
the mob; and that Mr. Henry M. Musgrave had read the riot act at 20
1.25.

The riotous mob assembled in front of the King's Arms inn.
Various attempts were made by the constabulary force (i.e. by the
very few who had made any attempt to do their duty) to take the
ringleaders into custody, but they were defeated by the mob. The 25
high constable Shaw and many others were knocked down and
abused.

. . . Mr Adey, the assistant poor law commissioner proceeded to
London to state the circumstances to the board of commissioners and
to procure assistance from the government . . . Eleven persons duly 30
appointed and summoned to attend to take the oath as special
constables and who neglected or refused to do so were fined. Another
precept, appointing more special constables in the several parishes in
the union was signed by 3 magistrates, and a summons for every
person so appointed to attend at the King's Arms inn, Ampthill, on 35
Tuesday morning at 9 o'clock was given to the constable of the
several parishes. The mob have dispersed at 7 o'clock, the magistrates
addjourned until Friday the 15th.

Bedfordshire Record Office PSA 1/4

5.15(c)   Daniel Adey's evidence

When was the riot? – At the beginning of the formation of the union
in the year 1835.

What was the origin of the riot? – The origin was the change of
the allowance system from money to bread, but the general feeling
against the introduction of the law was another cause, the men being 5
apprehensive of being shut up in the workhouse, and they stated to
me most distinctly (I was in the crowd for three hours, in the middle
of them, talking to them), that all they wanted was work; that was
their constant cry; one of the observations was this 'that the land was
in such a state that you might plough a furrow, and drag it from 10
Ampthill to Bedford', meaning that the land was so extremely
foul . . .

Have you heard . . . that there is any improvement in the
cultivation of the soil, arising from greater employment of the
labourers? – I believe there is no doubt at all of that . . . 15

You say you see no difference in their appearance; do you perceive
any difference in their disposition, in the feeling that exists, as
between the employer and the employed? – I should say that there
can be no doubt whatever upon the subject . . . that those people
now touch their hats to you as you pass; before they were always   20
sulky; four years back, if you passed them, they were generally sulky
looking people, and now they are civil and polite; I can perceive that
difference.

**Minutes of evidence before Select Committee on the Poor Law
Amendment Act, Parliamentary Papers, 1837–8, vol. xviii, pt II**

Questions

1   What were the causes of opposition to the new Poor Law according
to **5.14** and **5.15(c)**?
2   Using **5.15(a)–(c)** describe the causes and course of the Ampthill riot
in 1835. What were its consequences?
3   Neither petitions to parliament nor riots led to changes in the law.
Discuss.

In industrial areas the problem of poverty was different from that in rural
areas. Relief was seen as a temporary expedient to see the worker through
'hard times' and not as a permanent feature. Opposition was widespread
since the timing of implementation coincided with the first major crisis of
industrialisation from 1837 to 1841. Anti-Poor Law activity merged into
Chartism and soon lost whatever paternalist characteristics it possessed.

5.16   Richard Oastler

CHRISTIAN READER

Be not alarmed at the sound of the Title. I can not bless that, which
God and NATURE CURSE. The Bible being true, the Poor Law
Amendment Act is false! The Bible containing the will of God – this
accursed Act of Parliament embodies the will of Lucifer. It is the   5
Sceptre of Belial, establishing its sway in the Land of Bibles!!
DAMNATION; ETERNAL DAMNATION to the accursed Fiend!!
. . . I tell you deliberately, if I have the misfortune to be reduced to
poverty, That that man who dares to tear from me the wife whom
God has joined to me, shall, if I have it in my power, receive his   10

death at my hand! If I am ever confined in one of those hellish Poor
Law Bastiles, and my wife be torn from me, because I am poor, I
will, if it be possible, burn the whole pile down to the ground. This
will I do, if my case shall be thus tried, if I have the power; and
every man who loved his wife, and who is unstained by crime, will if   15
he can, do the same. – Further, I will not pay any tax imposed upon
me, under this Act . . .

Richard Oastler, *Damnation! Eternal Damnation to the Fiend-
begotten Coarser-Food New Poor Law*, 1837, frontispiece and p. 10

5.17 Blood and fire

The people were not going to stand this, and he would say, that
sooner than wife and husband, and father and son, should be
sundered and dungeoned and fed on 'skillee', – sooner than wife and
daughter should wear the prison dress – sooner than that – Newcastle
ought to be, and should be – one blaze of fire, with only one way to   5
put it out and that with the blood of all who supported this
abominable measure . . . He [Mr Stephens] was a revolutionist by
fire, he was a revolutionist by blood, to the knife, to the death. If an
unjust, unconstitutional and illegal parchment was carried in the
pockets of the Poor Law Commissioners, and handed over to be   10
slung on a musket, or a bayonet, and carried through their bodies by
an armed force . . . then it would be law for every man to have his
firelock, his cutlass, his sword, his pair of pistols, or his pike, and
every woman to have her pair of scissors, and for every child to have
its paper of pins and its box of needles . . . and let the men with a   15
torch in one hand and a dagger in the other, put to death any and all
who attempted to sever man and wife.

Speech by Revd J. R. Stephens in January 1838, printed in R. G.
Gammage, *History of the Chartist Movement*, 1854, pp. 64–5

5.18 'The Book of the Bastiles' 1841

But the paramount reason for publishing . . . was, the urgent
necessity in the present alarming crisis – a crisis mainly attributable
to the operation of such harsh, biting statutes as the New Poor-Law
– of calling the attention of the upper and middle classes to the

inhumanity, unchristianity, injustice and political and social danger of 5
the continued administration of the New Poor-Law Amendment Act
in England and Wales . . . Had there been no Poor Law, the name of
Chartism would never have been heard, nor Birmingham have been
heated with fire and fury, or Newport run red with the gore of
Britons from the hills. These are truisms that need no further parley. 10
That Rural Police, and increased taxation, are the 'Act's' necessary
assistants on the Government's side, and stack-firing, and the
manufacturing of pikes, its natural accompaniments on the side of the
governed . . . The New Poor-Law and good government and good
order cannot exist together: the former must and will destroy the 15
other two.

**G. R. Wythen Baxter, *The Book of the Bastiles*, 1841, pp. iii–iv – a
compendium of stories about the operation of the 1834 Act**

5.19   PUNCH'S PENCILLINGS. ——Nº. LXII.

THE "MILK" OF POOR-LAW "KINDNESS."

Punch, 1843

5.20 'Tremendous Sacrifice!'

George Cruickshank, from *Our Own Times*, 1846

Questions

1   How is the new Poor Law portrayed in an unfavourable light in documents **5.16** to **5.20**? How well do you think each succeeds?
2   In what ways was the opposition to the Poor Law in industrial areas paternalist in character? Why was early opposition paternalist?
3   Why was the new Poor Law never introduced fully into industrial Britain?
4   How cruel was the new Poor Law?

The 1834 Act has been seen as a major watershed dividing the parochial from the centralised administration of poverty. It has also been interpreted as a divide in social values, a change from paternalism to the pursuit of economy and efficiency. Poverty became politicised. But paternalistic values remained throughout Britain. Workhouses and unions predated 1834 and outdoor relief continued long after.

References

1   For a full discussion of this problem see G. Himmelfarb *The Idea of Poverty: England in the Early Industrial Age*, 1984, or if you do not feel up to reading her magisterial work look at the extract in *History Today*, April 1984
2   There are innumerable books on this subject of which A. Digby, 'The Poor Law in Nineteenth century England and Wales', *Historical Association*, 1982, is a manageable starter. D. Fraser (ed.), *The New Poor Law in the Nineteenth Century*, 1976, contains some important papers. J. D. Marshall, *The Old Poor Law 1795–1834*, 1968, and M. Rose, *The Relief of Poverty 1834–1914*, 1972, give a brief summary of the controversy
3   See N. C. Edsall, *The anti-Poor Law movement 1834–44*, Manchester, 1971
4   On conditions in the workhouse see N. Longmate, *The Workhouse*, 1974, and the more recent M. A. Crowther, *The Workhouse System 1834–1929*, 1982

6 Religion and education – liberation or social control?

High and low, cobblers, tinkers, hackney coachmen, men and maid servants, soldiers, tradesmen of all ranks, lawyers, physicians, gentlemen, Lords are as ignorant of the Creator of the World as Mohametans or Pagans. (*John Wesley, 1782*)

The necessity of going to church in procession with us on the anniversary, raises an honest ambition to get something decent to wear, and the churches on Sunday are now filled with very clean-looking women. (*Hannah More to William Wilberforce, 1791*)

In the first half of the nineteenth century the appeal of the Christian religion in much of England was in decline. The 1851 Religious Census made this plain. But religion could be dynamic, a source of liberation in earthly as well as spiritual terms. It could also be the symbol of social order and stability.

The reasons for the religious decline lay in the failure of the Established Church to respond adequately to the demands of the redistribution of population or, in Ireland, to a predominantly Catholic peasantry. Its parochial structure just could not cope with the increasingly urban nature of society. Not until long after the Anglican church-building programme began in 1818 were there enough places of worship for urban Anglicans. This problem of logistics was added to by the abuses of non-residence, pluralism and the Toryism of many clergymen, seriously weakening the position of the Church as a source of stability. This was accelerated by the move towards Wesleyan Methodism which was able to capitalise on Anglican weaknesses. But even here the clericalism, autocracy and Toryism of Wesleyan Methodism, personified by Jabez Bunting and continually re-iterated at Conference, led to secession and the establishment of more radical Methodist groupings – the Primitive Methodists and Methodist New Connexion.

Religion taught duty and obedience and was seen as fundamental to social order in this period of rapid change.

6.1   Wilberforce on Christianity and social order

There will be no capricious humours, no selfish tempers, no
moroseness, no discourtesy, no affected severity of deportment, no
peculiarity of language, no indolent neglect, no wanton breach, of the
ordinary forms or fashions of society . . . If he give offence, it will
only be where he dares not do otherwise; and if he falls into dis-   5
esteem or disgrace it shall not be chargeable to any conduct which is
justly dishonourable, or even to any unnecessary singularities on his
part, but to the false standard of estimation of a misjudging world
. . . In whatever class or order of society Christianity prevails, she
sets herself to rectify the particular faults, or if we would speak more   10
distinctly, to counteract the particular mode of selfishness to which
that class is liable. Affluence she teaches to be liberal and beneficent;
authority to bear its faculties with meekness, and to consider the
various cares and obligations belonging to its elevated station, as
being conditions upon which that station is conferred. Thus,   15
softening the glare of wealth, and moderating the insolence of power,
she renders the inequalities of the social state less galling to the lower
orders, whom also she instructs, in their turn, to be diligent, humble,
patient . . . and that it is their part faithfully to discharge its duties,
and contentedly to bear its inconveniences . . . Religion . . . affords   20
more satisfaction than all the expensive pleasures which are above the
poor man's reach; that in this view, however, the poor have the
advantage, and that if their superiors enjoy more abundant comforts,
they are also exposed to many temptations from which the inferior
classes are happily exempted . . . finally, that all human distinctions   25
will soon be done away, and the true followers of Christ will all, as
children of the same father, be alike admitted to the possession of the
same heavenly inheritance.

William Wilberforce, *A Practical View of Christianity*, 1797

6.2   How a Christian will never be a leveller

The true Christian will never be a leveller; will never listen to French
politics, or to French philosophy. He who worships God in spirit and
in truth will love the government and laws which protect him without
asking by whom they are administered. But let it not be imagined
that such characters will abound among the lower classes while the   5

higher by their Sunday parties, excursions and amusements and
vanities; by their neglect of public worship and their families show
that they feel not themselves, what perhaps they talk of, or
recommend for the poor.

Arthur Young, *An Enquiry into the State of the Public Mind*, 1798,
p. 25

6.3 The duty of a patient, 1840

John Bush, carpenter and Wheel-wright of Yarnton [Oxfordshire]
was admitted into this Infirmary Jan 1st, having crushed his hand; he
was discharged, cured Jan 22nd, upon which occasion a Thanksgiving
Paper was delivered to him, to give to the officiating Minister;
knowing him to be a bad man, I charged him to remember his duty   5
in this particular, and to attend Church to return thanks and to think
seriously of the accident.

He never delivered his Thanksgiving Paper, nor has he returned
Thanks.

I shall move on Wednesday that he be put upon the list of   10
Disorderly Patients, and that he be not permitted to have any of the
dispensations of this Infirmary either as an In or an Out Patient
except in the single case of dangerous Accident.

The 'General Visitors' Book', 3 February 1840, Radcliffe Infirmary

6.4 An employer addresses workers whom he had locked out for eight weeks in 1836

While the foreman gets his 30*s* or 40*s*, the striker whose labour is
more severe only received 20*s* or 30*s*; while he that has served an
apprenticeship obtained his 20*s* to 30*s*, the learner and the mere
labourer gets his 10*s* to 18*s*. In all these cases the God of nature has
established a just and equitable law, which man has no right to   5
disturb; when he ventures to do so, it is always certain that he,
sooner or later, meets with a corresponding punishment. That law is
the natural operation of things, and in proportion as man, by trickery,
manoeuvre or an abuse of power, violates this law of nature and
equity, in the same degree does he receive his reward. Thus when   10
masters audaciously combine, that they may effectually oppress their

servants, they insult the Majesty of heaven and bring down the curse of God upon themselves, while on the other hand, when servants unite to exort from their employers that share of profit which of right belongs to the master, they violate the laws of equity . . . The master manufacturers of England were foremost in their struggles to secure that glorious reform in Parliament which I doubt not will end in the moral and political regeneration of the world . . . singlehanded, you must submit to receive merely the share of profits which the God of nature assigns you.

William Ibbotson, *Address to the Workmen in the File Trade*, 1836, Sheffield Library Local Pamphlets, vol. vi

Questions

1   What arguments do documents 6.1 and 6.2 put forward to explain the intimate relationship between Christianity and social stability?
2   Given the changing nature of society and economy, how valid do you think these arguments in 6.1 and 6.2 would be to the following?
    (i) a working miner
    (ii) an unemployed weaver
    (iii) a member of the middle class
    (iv) a wealthy landowner
    Account for your conclusions.
3   How can documents 6.3 and 6.4 be used to establish the principle of reciprocal social obligations?
4   Christianity justified inequality. Explain with reference to the documents [6.1–6.4].
5   In late eighteenth- and early nineteenth-century Britain the most important function of religion was teaching obedience to the established order. Discuss.

Nowhere was the role of religion more evident and more controversial than in the realm of education for the labouring population. Should the function of education be obedience, duty or liberation? And what should actually be taught – reading, writing, and thinking?

6.5   Putting people in their place

The ignorance of the poor affords their masters the best security of
their unremitting Utility, Faithfulness and Obedience. That to
instruct them in Reading and Writing generally puffs them with
Arrogance, Vanity, Self Conceit and . . . unfits them for the menial
stations which Providence has allotted them.

J. Fawel, *The Principles of Sound Policy*, 1785

6.6   Anglican attitudes, 1802

We are merely to give them an entrance into a life of daily labour,
well fortified with the principles of duty (he warned his hearers); all
beyond that may puff up their tender minds, or entice them into a
way of life of no benefit to the Publick and ensnaring to themselves.
Accomplishments that are useful and becoming in one rank of life are   5
neither becoming nor safe in another. The Church Catechism
strongly inculcated, habits of piety and industry and of attendance
upon religious worship with a sense of their duty in the same, and
means of receiving instruction and advantage from it; these, together
with skill in the manual operations which they are destined to   10
perform may, I believe, be reckoned the sum of the education
necessary for the poor.

Sermon preached by John Randolph, Bishop of Oxford, at the
Church of St Mary le Bow, 20 May 1802, p. 19

6.7   Methodist attitudes, 1802

I have had an opportunity now for twenty years of observing the
amazing utility of Sunday Schools, in London, Manchester and
Liverpool and various other towns and villages, and I can speak with
truth that their salutary influence has been unspeakable. Multitudes
of poor untaught children who used to spend the Lord's day in   5
associating together, prompting and instructing the other, the more
grown-up the younger in vice and wickedness such as swearing, lying,
pilfering and all sorts of mischief; but by the above humane
institution are happily reclaimed, many of them have become very
useful members of Society. And this more particularly so where all   10

the teachers act from principle and bestow their labour gratis, as is done in all the Methodist Connexion. The children are taught to read and write, and likewise their morals are attended to: to be diligent and industrious, to behave with respect to their superiors: to avoid lying, stealing, speaking vain words, and to be true and just in all   15
their dealings. But altogether the teachers teach gratis, yet considerable expense is unavoidable, as the rent of the room, benches, books, pens and ink &c. Hoping the inhabitants of Oldbury and its environs will see the utility of this laudable design and do all in their powers to support it.   20

T. TAYLOR, Birmingham, 1802

Revd T. Taylor, 1802, quoted in M. Edwards, *After Wesley*, 1935, pp. 105–6

6.8   A Welsh view, 1847

The universality of these schools, and the large proportion of persons attending them who take part in their government, have very generally familiarized the people with some of the more ordinary terms and methods of organization such as committee, secretary and so forth . . . these schools satisfy the gregarious sociability which   5
animates the Welsh towards each other . . . every man, woman and child feels comfortably at home in them. It is all among neighbours and equals. Whatever ignorance is shown here, whatever mistakes are made, whatever strange speculations are started, there are no superiors to smile and open their eyes . . . Whatever Sunday-schools   10
may be as places of instruction, they are real fields of mental activity. The Welsh working-man rouses himself for them. Sunday is to him more than a day of bodily rest and devotion. It is his best chance, all the week through, of showing himself in his own character. He marks his sense of it by a suit of clothes regarded with a feeling hardly less   15
sabbatical than the day itself. I do not remember to have seen an adult in rags in a single Sunday-school throughout the present district. They always seemed to me better dressed on Sundays than the same classes in England.

Report of the Commissioners of Inquiry into the State of Education in Wales, vol. i, p. 6

Questions

1   According to documents **6.5** to **6.8**, what was the function of
     education? In what ways do the emphases of these documents differ?
2   How did education lead to 'improvement'?
3   Compare the Anglican with the Methodist attitude to education [**6.6**
     and 6.7].
4   The Sunday school was the most important source of social stability
     in the early nineteenth century. Discuss.

Any statement on the role of the Established Church as a source of order
was unnecessary. However, despite the fact that Methodism was always a
loyalist movement, its critics frequently represented it otherwise:

sedition and atheism were the real objects of their institutions.

a system which tended to overthrow Church and State.

Methodists are unfavourable to our civil as well as ecclesiastical
institutions.

As a result Methodism, especially under the influence of Jabez Bunting,
became ultra-Tory in its perspective, stating its support for the State
whenever possible.

6.9   Conference 1812

The well-known loyalty of our Societies, their dutiful attachment to
their King and Country . . . Societies are uncontaminated with that
spirit of insubordination, violence and cruelty which had caused so
much distress and misery . . . (alarm must be given) lest any of our
dear people should be drawn away by the dissimulation of evil-   5
disposed men. We proclaim loudly and earnestly, 'For the Lord and
the King; and meddle not with them that are given to change'. Avoid
them, come not near them.

Methodist Magazine, 1812, p. 720

6.10   Conference 1813

We cannot but feel a strong attachment to our civil constitution, and
a confirmed regard for our rulers, who have on all occasions,
discovered a liberal spirit towards us as people. We are therefore still
resolved to recommend both by word and deed, the duty of fearing
God and honouring the King.

Methodist Magazine, 1813, p. 720

6.11   Conference 1843

[some of the bretheren] were commendably active in the protection of
property and the restoration of order . . . history proves they have
hitherto been . . . faithful to the throne, constitution and laws of our
beloved country, the exemplars of order, loyalty and patriotism.

Conference Minutes, 1843

6.12   Attitude to Luddism

In 1812, when the infatuated populace of the West Riding of
Yorkshire in the madness and wickedness of their folly visited like
prowling wolves the abodes of their neighbours, exciting the most
fearful apprehensions for personal safety, demolishing property and
destroying life, the Methodist ministers did not shrink from the duty   5
they owed to their country, but publicly and from house to house,
laboured to counteract the influence of wicked and mischievous men.
I have no wish to underrate the influence of the truly pious of other
denominations yet . . . it is on record as a historical fact that
Methodist ministers were, I believe, the only ministers of religion as   10
a body who made a declaration of their sentiments at the awful crisis
in an address to their Societies, in which they said, 'We look at the
principles which have given birth to this state of things with the
utmost horror, principles which are alike destructive to the happiness
of poor and rich'.

**Anon., 'Reasons for Methodism' in a letter to the Bishop of Exeter,
1834, p. 28**

6.13   After Peterloo 1819

We desire to record our strong and decided disapprobation of the
tumultuous assemblies which have lately been witnessed in many
parts of the country, in which large masses of people have been
irregularly collected. There have been wild and delusive political
theories, and violent and inflammatory declamations which bring the   5
Government into contempt. From all such public meetings the
members of the Methodist Societies are asked to abstain. Ministers
are asked to warn people against private political associations illegally
organised: any person connected with our body persisting after due
admonition in identifying himself with the factious and disloyal shall   10
forthwith be expelled from the Society . . . The Committee [of
Privileges] have received with cordial satisfaction assurances of the
loyal spirit and demeanour of our Societies in general and devoutly
trust that at this crisis, as on several similar occasions in former years,
the influence of Christian principles and discipline on the poorer   15
classes of our Society will be found highly beneficial in
discountenancing the machinations of the ill-disposed, and in leading
the suffering poor of our manufacturing districts, whose distress the
Committee sincerely commiserate, to bear their privations with
patience and to seek relief not in the schemes of agitation and crime,   20
but in reliance on Divine Providence, and in continued prayer for the
blessing of God on our country and on themselves.

T. P. Bunting, *Life of Jabez Bunting*, vol. ii, p. 188

Questions

1   What was the basis for Methodist support for government and the
state as shown in documents **6.10** to **6.13**?
2   Why do you think that the Methodist leadership adopted this
viewpoint?
3   How did the Methodist leadership react to radical agitation between
1810 and 1850? Did that response change?
4   The Methodist leadership, particularly under Jabez Bunting, was out
of touch with much grassroot opinion. This profoundly affected the
development of Methodism in the first half of the nineteenth
century. Discuss.

5   Why was Jabez Bunting such a central figure in the development of
     Methodism?
6   Methodism prevented revolution in the first half of the nineteenth
     century. How have historians disagreed on this?
7   Just how 'neutral' were the Methodists?

Until 1833 the Churches financed their own voluntary schools. These
were run by two main religious societies: the British and Foreign Society
for Nonconformists and the National Society for the Anglicans. These
institutions suffered from their over-zealous approach to religion and their
antagonism for each other. They were undecided precisely what should be
taught and lacked trained staff. The quality of education suffered
accordingly.

6.14   The work of the National Society for Anglicans in the 1830s

What progress has the society made during the 23 years it has
existed, and what is the extent of its connexion at present? . . . In
1813 there were 239 schools in union, containing 40,484 children:
such were the effects of the first operations of the society . . . in
1831, it appears there were 10,965 schools in union and acting upon   5
the same principle, having in them under education 740,000 children;
but as no returns were received from many places, it was considered
requisite to add to the above number an estimate of the number
educated in those places, by which the number of children educated
under the Church of England was brought up to 900,000.

**Evidence of William Cotton, Parliamentary Papers, 1834, vol. ix, p. 9,
1876, printed with returns in G. M. Young and W. D. Handcock,
English Historical Documents, vol. xii(1), 1956, pp. 845–7**

6.15   Urban education in the 1830s

Your committee now turn to the state of Education in the large
manufacturing and seaport towns, where the population has rapidly
increased within the present century; they refer for particulars to the
evidence taken before them, which appears to bear out the following
results: 5

1st. That the kind of education given to the children of the working classes is lamentably deficient.

2nd. That it extends (bad as it is) to but a small proportion of those who ought to receive it.

3rd. That without some strenuous and persevering efforts be made 10 on the part of Government, the greatest evils to all classes may follow from this neglect.

. . . The general result of all these towns is, that about one in 12 receives some sort of daily instruction, but only about one in 24 an education likely to be useful. In Leeds, only one in 41; in 15 Birmingham, one in 38; in Manchester, one in 35 . . . Evidence taken . . . describe[d] in strong terms the misery and crime likely to arise from the neglected education of the children of the working classes in populous places . . . this cause (embracing the want of religion and moral training) is to be chiefly attributed to the great increase of 20 criminals and consequently of cost to the country.

Select Committee on the Education of the Poorer Classes, Parliamentary Papers, 1837–8, vol. vii, pp. vii–ix

6.16   Education in Sheffield, December 1840

Sunday schools

Type of School	No. of Schools	No. of Scholars
Church of England	38	3901
Wesleyan Methodist	25	4034
Roman Catholic	2	181
Independent/Calvinist	18	2394
Unitarian	2	226
New Connexion Methodist	5	1093
Methodist Association	4	280
Primitive Methodist	2	169
Baptist	4	626
TOTAL	100	12904

Public day schools

Type of School	No. of Schools	No. of Scholars
Endowed	8	407
Church of England	24	3345
Wesleyan Methodist	5	700
Lancastrian	2	1114
Roman Catholic	2	133
TOTAL	41	5699

Summary of pupils

In public day schools	5699
In private schools	4459
In infant schools	797
TOTAL	10,955

The population of the parish of Sheffield in 1841 was 112 492, of whom at least half would be below twenty years.

G. C. Holland, *Vital Statistics of Sheffield*, 1843, p. 221

Questions

1   How are the conclusions of document **6.14** on numbers in schools brought into question by documents **6.15** and **6.16**?
2   Why did the Select Committee believe that lack of education could have dire social consequences [**6.15**]? What does this say about its attitudes to the role of education?
3   What information can be 'squeezed' from document **6.16** about education in Sheffield?
4   It does not matter how many children went to school as the quality of education was poor. Discuss.
5   'Education mattered little to large sections of the working population'. 'Knowledge gives power'. Discuss these two statements.

There were two main consequences of the attitudes of the Churches to society. On the one hand there was a jockeying for position between Nonconformity and Anglicanism best exemplified in the debates on the education clauses of the Factories Bill of 1843. On the other hand their conservatism, graphically seen in the Reform crisis in 1832 and in the autocracy of Bunting, 'The Methodist Pope', led to growing anti-clericalism. Many people turned away from the established religions. The 1851 Religious Census established the depth of religious apathy and antagonism.

6.17(a)   The 1843 Factories Bill: Sir James Graham introduces the Bill, 28 February 1843

Parliament has dealt with the subject of education as regards factory children, but in so imperfect and unsatisfactory a manner, as almost to render nugatory the measures which have been adopted. The Legislature has imposed upon manufacturers the necessity of giving the children in their employment some education, but it has been   5
omitted to make some provision with regard to the quality or the degree of that education . . . Now the principle hitherto enforced by the Committee of Education in distributing the sum annually placed at their disposal by Parliament has been to make no advance of money for the building of a school, unless two-thirds of the whole   10
sum required has been raised by subscription . . . It, therefore, appears to me indisputably necessary to adhere to the principle of making advances from the public fund only in proportion to some given amount raised by private subscription; but . . . I am bound to declare that as regards the poorer districts some relaxation of the   15
existing rule of proportion is imperatively called for. I propose, therefore, that in any districts where the regulations with respect to the education of factory children shall be in force, and in which local subscriptions, aided by public grants, may be inadequate to the erection of schools, the inhabitants shall be enabled to procure a loan,   20
to the extent of one-third of the cost of the building . . . Then comes the question 'How are these district schools to be managed?' I propose that they shall be managed by trusts . . . The general management of the schools will be under the control of the trustees; they will have the power of appointing the master, subject to the   25
approval of the bishop of the diocese as to his competency to give religious instruction to members of the Established Church. The Holy Scriptures are to be taught daily, but no child will be required to receive instruction in the Catechism of the Church of England or

attend the Established Church whose parents object on religious   30
grounds.

Hansard, Series 3, vol. lxvii, 77–88

6.17(b)   Debate on the Amended Bill, 1 May 1843

The Petitions which have been presented against those clauses of the
Factories Bill to which I am about to advert have been numerous
almost without a parallel . . . I am at once ready to admit, that
amongst the great Dissenting bodies of this country there does prevail
at the present moment a very unanimous feeling against the   5
educational clauses of this bill . . . No man in this House can more
strongly deprecate the introduction of religious topics into our
debates as I do . . . how is it that in the heart of this very country, in
this fair England, there is so great a mass of ignorance and infidelity
– infidelity arising not from the perversions of the reasoning powers,   10
but from want of knowledge . . .?

Hansard, Series 3, vol. lxviii, 1104–8

6.18   1832

There is a strong popular feeling against the political opinions of the
clergy, particularly of the bishops and other dignitaries among them
. . . Hear the cry with which the bishops in particular are now
assailed in every part of the kingdom, and most loudly in the great
manufacturing districts. Whence comes the special bitterness with   5
which they, above all the other anti-reforming peers, are everywhere
attacked? Whence the hatred with which the whole order of the
clergy is sometimes attacked? Is it not because the people have never
been made to feel the full amount of the goods which an established
church may and ought to effect . . .? Is it not because in our large   10
manufacturing towns the church has allowed thousands and tens of
thousands of its members to grow up in misery and in ignorance . . .?
Was it fit to wait for money enough to build an expensive church,
rather than licence the first room, or the first court-yard that could
be found, wherever the inhabitants of the parish become too   15
numerous or too remote to attend the Parish Church?

Thomas Arnold, 'Thirteen Letters addressed to the Editor of the
Sheffield Courant on our social conditions', Sheffield, 1832

6.19   An Anglican view

[The parish of St Philip's] contained 24,000 labourers and mechanics
(about one fourth of the entire population of Sheffield); there is one
church; and until very recently only one clergyman. The church
contains 800 free sittings, and accomodates 1,200 in the pews . . .
Now surely it will be thought, in such a teeming population, the   5
accommodation, especially the free sittings, will be eagerly sought
after. Alas, the reverse is true. The wealthier classes, in tolerable
numbers, are found occupying the pews; but the free seats are too
often thinly tenanted. To what shall we attribute this indifference to
Divine ordinances? . . . the prevailing reason, I am assured, is the   10
force of inveterate habit . . . they tread in the steps of their fathers,
and are neither impressed with the obligation, nor feel the desire, of
obtaining religious instruction . . . The moral condition of the people
is precisely what might be anticipated . . . Can it be surprising that
the profane doctrines and licentious practices of the Socialists, so   15
congenial to the animal appetites of the ignorant, find numerous
abettors? It is quite natural that in such a population, the demagogue
and political firebrand will find abundant materials for sedition,
reason and rebellion . . . There is indisputable evidence, that the
ramifications of the late Chartist conspiracy were deep and numerous   20
in this district.

**John Livesey, 'Mechanics' Churches – a Letter to Sir Robert Peel on
Church Extension in the populous towns and Manufacturing
Districts', Sheffield Library Local Pamphlets, vol. ciii**

Questions

1   Why were the debates on the Factories Bill in 1843 so vehement?
2   What did Dissenters fear would be the result of the Bill and was that
     fear justified?
3   Use document **6.18** to discuss why anti-clerical feeling rose to such a
     peak in 1832.
4   Why, according to document **6.19**, was the Anglican Church
     alienating the labouring population?
5   The 1840s saw religious conflict rise to an intensity unparalleled in
     the first half of the nineteenth century. Discuss.

6.20(a)   The 1851 Census – the main facts

The great facts which appear to me to have been elicited by this
inquiry are, – that even taking the accommodation provided by all
the sects, including the most extravagant, unitedly, there are
1,644,734 inhabitants of England who, if all who might attend
religious services were willing to attend, would not be able, on   5
account of insufficient room, to join in public worship: that this
deficiency prevails almost exclusively in towns, especially large towns:
that, if these 1,644,734 persons are to be deprived of all excuse for
non-attendance, there must be at least as many additional sittings
furnished, equal to about 2,000 churches and chapels . . . Further, it   10
appears that as many as 5,288,294 persons able to attend, are every
Sunday absent from religious services, for all of whom there is
accomodation for at least one service: that neglect like this, in spite of
opportunities for worship, indicates the insufficiency of any mere
addition to the number of religious buildings: that the greatest   15
difficulty is to fill the churches when provided; and that this can only
be accomplished by a great addition to the number of efficient,
earnest, religious teachers, clerical or lay, by whose persuasions the
reluctant population might be won.

Parliamentary Papers, 1852–3, vol. lxxxix

6.20(b)   Nonconformity

The most numerous religious bodies, next to the established church,
are the Wesleyan Methodists, the Independents or Congregationalists
and the Baptists . . . The WESLEYAN METHODISTS are found
in greatest force in Cornwall, Yorkshire, Lincolnshire, Derbyshire,
Durham and Nottinghamshire; their fewest numbers are in   5
Middlesex, Surrey, Sussex, Essex, Warwickshire and Hertfordshire.
The INDEPENDENTS flourish most in South Wales, North Wales,
Essex, Dorsetshire, Monmouthshire and Suffolk; least in
Northumberland, Durham, Hertfordshire and Worcestershire. The
BAPTISTS are strongest in Monmouthshire, South Wales,   10
Huntingdonshire, Bedfordshire, Northamptonshire, Leicestershire
and Buckinghamshire; weakest in Cumberland, Northumberland,
Westmorland, Cornwall, Staffordshire and Lancashire.

Parliamentary Papers, 1852–3, vol. lxxxix, pp. cxliii–clxv

6.20(c)   The 1851 Religious Census – a sample

Bedfordshire*

Denomination	Places of worship	Potential total attendance	a.m.	p.m.	evg.
Anglican	133	42557	20559	24905	5606
Baptist**	55	14902	9070	8622	8164
Brethren	1	500	70	40	50
Catholic***	1	80	80	—	80
Independents	19	5827	3149	2691	3430
Jews	1	20	—	—	—
Mormans	3	240	90	140	122
Wesleyans	78	16736	6807	11017	12839
Primitive Methodists	18	2490	783	1801	2603
Moravians	3	840	652	264	777
Roman Catholic	1	21	50	20	—
Society of Friends	3	622	124	63	22
Others	11	3021	1917	2046	1577
TOTALS	327	87856	43351	51609	35270

 * total population of Bedfordshire – 124 478
 ** figures for Baptist combine those of General, Particular and not defined
*** Catholic and Apostolic church

Modified from the table in the printed volume of the Religious Census, Parliamentary Papers, 1852–3, vol. lxxxix, p. cxcv

Questions

1   What are the main causes of concern identified in document **6.20(a)**? In what ways did document **6.19** identify this concern ten years earlier?

2   Explain the geographical distribution of Nonconformity identified in document **6.20(b)**.

3   Explain the nature of religious belief in Bedfordshire in 1851 [**6.20(c)**]. In what ways does it conform to the national picture and in what way does it differ?

4   Why did the conclusions of the Religious Census make such an impact on mid nineteenth-century society?

5   Religion declined as a force for social order in this period. Discuss.

The first half of the nineteenth century was a period of almost continual retreat for the Established Church. It lost its political exclusiveness in 1828–9. Events in 1832 increased its unpopularity. The defeat of the 1843 Factories Bill destroyed whatever hopes the Church retained of being the sole vehicle for the education of the people. But despite damaging losses it survived. Wesleyan Methodism should have been able to build on the weakness of Anglicanism. It did. But institutionalised by Bunting and others it lacked its former 'enthusiasm' – the result was internal tension and schism. The message of Church and Chapel, though still influential, offered few answers to the problems of industrialised and urbanised society. People just stopped attending on Sundays.

7 Class and rank – perceptions of society

The bond of attachment is broken, there is no longer the generous bounty which calls forth a grateful and honest and confiding dependence.

Robert Southey, *Colloquies on the Progress and Prospects of Society*, 1829, p. 47

You are for reducing the community to two classes: Masters and Slaves.

William Cobbett, *Political Register*, 14 April 1821

There is no community . . . there is aggregation . . . modern society acknowledges no neighbours.

New Statistical Account of Scotland, 1845, vol. vii, p. 332

The changes in the economy and particularly the growth of towns meant new patterns of lifestyle and work. The old social values were questioned. The notion of 'class' intruded into hierarchical society, which had been based upon 'ranks' or 'orders' or, when economic groupings were identified, 'interests'. This change meant not just a different social structure but a different system of values. The documents in this final chapter are concerned with the contemporary debate on these issues. They illustrate the confused, unordered nature of that debate.

7.1 Change in perspective

The physical order of communities, in which the production of the necessaries of subsistence is the first want and chief occupation, has in our case been rapidly inverted, and in lieu of agricultural supremacy, a vast and overtopping structure of manufacturing wealth and population has been substituted . . . To this extraordinary revolution, I doubt not, may be traced much of the bane and many of the blessings incidental to our condition – the growth of an opulent

5

commercial and a numerous, restless and intelligent operative class; sudden alternations of prosperity and depression – of internal quiet and violent political excitement; extremes of opulence and destitution; 10 the increase of crime; conflicting claims of capital and industry; the spread of an imperfect knowledge, that agitates and unsettles the old without having definitely settled the new foundations; clashing and independent opinions on most public questions, with other anomalies peculiar to our existing but changeful social existence.

John Wade, *History of the Middle and Working Classes*, 1833, p. 1

The 'old' values are represented in an imaginary conversation between weaver and master told by Samuel Bamford.

7.2

It is not honest – it is not Christian like – it is not wise. Let us try this vaunted principle, William, by the test of honesty – by the test 'Do thou unto others as thou wouldst they should do unto thee', and there is no better test of right and wrong under heaven. Suppose thou and thy family were distressed from want of employment and   5 thou came to me asking for work – and I, knowing thy situation, purchased thy labour 'at the cheapest rate at which I could get it', and sold it again at the dearest, putting the profit screwed out of thy necessities into my pocket – suppose I did so, – should I be acting like a Christian? – like an honest, conscientious man?

Samuel Bamford, *Early Days*, 1849, p. 122

7.3 Power and public opinion

The only means by which the classes of society can be defined, in a community where the laws are equal, is from the amount of property, either real or personal, possessed by individuals. As long as freedom and civilisation exist, property is so entirely the only power that no other means, or choice is left of distinguishing the several classes,   5 than by the amount of property belonging to the individuals of which they are formed . . . The extent or power of public opinion . . . resolves itself into the question whether . . . a community is possessed of an extensive middle class of society, when compared to a

lower class; for the advantages called requisites for public opinion,   10
cannot exist without a proportionate middle class . . . In every
community or state where public opinion becomes powerful or has
influence, it appears that the form of government becomes liberal in
the exact proportion as the power of public opinion increases . . .
Machinery creates wealth, which augments the middle class, which   15
gives strength to public opinion; consequently, to allude to the
extension of machinery is to account for the increase of the middle
class of society . . . That the results arising from the improvement of
machinery and its increase, are almost beyond the grasp of the human
mind to define, may seem probable from the change that has and is   20
daily taking place in the world.

**W. A. Mackinnon, *On the Rise, Progress and Present State of Public
Opinion in Great Britain and other Parts of the World*, 1828, pp. 2,
6–7, 10**

7.4 Conflict

Since the steam Engine has concentrated men into particular localities
– has drawn together the population into dense masses – and since an
imperfect education has enlarged, and to some degree distorted their
views, union is become easy and from being so closely packed,
simultaneous action is readily excited. The organisation of these   5
[working class] societies is now so complete that they form an
'imperium in imperio' of the most obnoxious description . . . Labour
and capital are coming into collision – the operative and the master
are at issue, and the peace, and well-being of the Kingdom are at
stake.

**Peter Gaskell to Lord Melbourne, 16 April 1834, Home Office Papers
40/32, quoted in A. Briggs, *The Language of Class in Early
Nineteenth-Century England*.**

7.5 Hazlitt on class

If we take away the character of the people of this country, or of any
large proportion of them, there is no degree of turpitude or injustice
that we may not introduce into the measures and treatment which we
consider as most fit for them. To legislate wisely, and for the best, it

is necessary that we should think as well, and not as ill, as possible,   5
of those for whom we legislate; or otherwise we shall soon reduce
them to the level of our own theories. To treat men as brute beasts in
our speculations, to encourage ourselves to treat them as such in our
practice; and that is the way to make them what we pretend to
believe they are . . . And when we see the lower classes of the   10
English people uniformly singled out as marks for the malice and
servility of a certain description of writers – when we see them
studiously separated, like a degraded caste, from the rest of the
community, with scarcely the attributes and faculties of the species
allowed them – nay, when they are thrust lower in the scale of   15
humanity than the same classes of any other nation in Europe –
though it is to these very classes that we owe the valour of our naval
and military heroes, the industry of our artisans and labouring
mechanics, and all that we have been told, again and again, elevates
us above every other nation in Europe . . . when we see every   20
existing evil derived from this unfortunate race, and every possible
vice ascribed to them – when we are accustomed to hear the poor,
the uninformed, the friendless, put, by tacit consent, out of the pale
of society – when their faults and wretchedness are exaggerated with
eager impatience, and still greater impatience is shown at every   25
expression of a wish to amend them – when they are familiarly
spoken of as a sort of vermin only fit to be hunted down, and
exterminated at the discretion of their betters: – we know pretty well
what to think, both of the disinterestedness of the motives which give
currency to this jargon, and of the wisdom of the policy which should   30
either sanction, or suffer itself to be influenced by its suggestions.

William Hazlitt 'Capital Punishments', *The Edinburgh Review*, **July
1821**

Questions

1   Identify the different perspectives of the impact of change contained
    in documents **7.1** to **7.5**.
2   What conflicts do documents **7.1** and **7.4** identify? Account for their
    differences.
3   Samuel Bamford and William Hazlitt identify different sets of social
    values. Explain this with reference to documents **7.2** and **7.5**.
4   John Wade writes of both 'the bane' and 'the blessings' of the new
    society [**7.1, lines 6–7**]. What do you think he meant by this?

5   In document 7.3 Mackinnon pegs class divisions to the distribution
     of property. Why did he do this and what effects did he think this
     had?
6   The problem for the historian of social change in this period is not
     the historical record but the contemporary meaning of the language
     used. Discuss.

It is in writings by churchmen that perhaps the clearest expressions of the
values of the 'old' society are to be found.

7.6

> The happy people of this kingdom enjoy the best security: where the
> interests of individuals are so connected, that material changes must
> affect the whole community: where the elevated situations, which
> wealth or power give, must be supported by the industry and labour
> of the indigent; and where they, on the other hand, receive protection 5
> and comfort from those, whose station they do materially uphold.
>
> **George Pelham, Bishop of Bristol, 'A Sermon Preached Before the
> Lords Spiritual and Temporal . . . February 26 1806', 1806**

7.7

> Every exertion to which civilisation can be traced proceeds, directly
> or indirectly, from its effects; either from the actual desire of having a
> family, or the pressing obligation of providing for one, or from the
> necessity of rivalling the efforts produced by the operation of these
> motives in others . . . [The Creator desired that] the human race   5
> should be uniformly brought into a state in which they are forced to
> exert and improve their powers: the lowest rank, to obtain support;
> the one next in order, to escape from the difficulties immediately
> beneath it; and all the classes upwards, either to keep their level,
> while they are pressed on each side by rival industry, or to raise   10
> themselves above the standard of their birth by useful exertion of
> their activity, or by successful cultivation of their natural powers.
>
> **J. B. Summner, *A Treatise On the Records of The Creation . . .*,
> 1816, vol. ii, pp. 132–3**

7.8   A weakening of the bonds

The lower orders of our countrymen will be forced to herd together
in towns still more completely than at present, out of the reach of
that kindly intercourse with their superiors, which ought to elevate
and improve the character of both parties. What little yet remains of
the connexion of the country gentlemen with a respectful and   5
attached peasantry will be sacrificed to a low and sordid calculation of
the profit to be derived from a transfer of the burthen of their relief;
it will be succeeded by a selfish and retired luxury on one side, and
the turbulence and lawless violence of the lazaroni and the other.

**Henry Phillpotts, A letter to the Right Honourable William Sturges
Bourne M.P. on a Bill . . . 'To Amend the Laws Respecting the
Settlement of the Poor', Durham, 1819, pp. 21–2**

7.9

The Almighty has given to his creatures different faculties and
endowments, both of mind and body. There must be the
Philosopher, the Statesman; the Artizan; and . . . at the same time,
the hewers of wood and the drawers of water. On the combined
operation of all, grounded in the conviction of mutual interest and   5
utility, depends the proper working, and the harmony, of the great
machine of the world.

G. H. Law, *Charge*, 1831, pp. 16–17

7.10   The eternal balance

Society is in fact a piece of machinery, disposed with consummate art
and contrivance, of which the several parts are so skilfully
interwoven, with such die proportion and reference to one another, as
to provide compensation for the defects and imperfections of all, and
minister to their preservation and safety. How beautiful the   5
arrangement by which the calm prudence of age and the ardent
activity of youth, the powerful engines of man and the amiable
qualities of the softer sex, are wrought into one harmonious system,
in which the rich and the poor, the mean and the mighty, the wisdom
that plans and the labour that executes, have each their separate   10

place, their several interests, and yet are so closely connected, that no member can suffer without some injury to others.

William Howley, 'A Sermon Preached at the Fifty-Second Anniversary of the Royal Humane Society . . . 9th April 1826', pp. 8–9

7.11

We look, it may be, every Sunday, at our well-filled churches, and we forget, for the moment, in the presence of those we see, the multitudes we see not; whose misery, as well as sin, whom want of room, want of clothes, indolence, neglect or utter wretchedness, are shutting out from our fellowship, and severing from civilization and   5 religion. Yet there they surely are. In all our great towns thin walls separate luxury from starvation. The two classes live in absolute ignorance of each other: there are no points of contact between them; the two streams nowhere intermingle: selfish respectability degrades one set; whilst misery and recklessness, which soon turn to vice and   10 wickedness, weigh down the other.

Samuel Wilberforce, *Charge*, 1844, pp. 15–16

7.12

Charge them that are rich in this world, that they do good, that they be rich in good works, ready to distribute, willing to communicate.

In a world like ours, there will always be occasion for this employment of wealth. There will always be some whom sudden reverses and unforeseen changes reduce to poverty. There will always   5 be children whose parents have been prematurely taken from them. There will always be widows suffering under a double loss, the loss of the means of subsistence as well as the means of happiness. There will always be many naked to be clothed, many hungry to be fed, many sick and afflicted to be relieved . . .

J. B. Summner, *Christian Charity, Its Obligations and Objects*, 1847, p. 22

7.13   Frustration

I cannot help remarking in this place, that the Country is now ruled
by Lawyers; originally the Clergy had an undue influence, and will
again, should the Catholic Religion obtain; but now they are utterly
unable to defend themselves. If they are injured in their property or
in their reputation, they may have recourse to the Law, and lose their   5
time, temper and money, and get laughed at in the bargain.

I am tied hands and feet, and placed in a pillory to be pelted at by
Methodists, Catholics, Colliers; and have moreover a combination of
worthless Farmers and an overbearing Woman with an unprincipled
Steward to contend with; who wishes to drive me by ill-usage from   10
the situation I occupy, that her Son-in-Law may step into it.

John Skinner, Diary, 7 April 1825, *Journal of a Somerset Rector 1803–
1834*, OUP, 1984, p. 283

For Skinner, rector of Camerton in Somerset since 1800, the torment
became too great and in 1839 he killed himself.

Questions

1   Using documents **7.6** to **7.12** identify the main features of the 'old'
      social values. Were they purely functional?
2   Compare and comment on documents **7.7** and **7.11**.
3   How do documents **7.8** and **7.11** explain the weakening of the system
      of dependence? What impact did this have?
4   'A system of reciprocal obligations'. 'A society of conflicting
      interests.' Discuss these statements.
5   How does John Skinner's prognosis [**7.13**] compare with documents
      7.8 and **7.11**?

As people moved away from the Established Church so the strength of
dependency declined.

7.14   The Welsh experience

The landlords are most of them of the old Church and King school –
the tenantry are almost all Dissenters, with a spice of the fanaticism
of the Covenanters about them. Still there is – or rather has been – a
sort of feudal deference existing between the parties – but I suspect it

to be the result of habit, rather than of feeling resulting from   5
conviction, and which may readily be put aside on a change of
circumstances. There is moreover another class more powerful
perhaps than even the Landlord – and this is the Preacher – and the
great bulk of the population are as much in their hands of their
priests.

William Day to G. C. Lewis, 9 July 1843, Home Office 45/1611

Questions

1   In Wales, Scotland and Ireland alienation from the established order
     had a religious basis. Discuss.
2   Habit or conviction. Which do you find the more satisfactory
     explanation for the system of deference and why?

It was, however, in the burgeoning towns that the bonds of dependency
were either non-existent or extremely weak. It was here that the 'class'
idea was to have the greatest impact.

7.15   'One of the oppressed'

I have told you that the evils under which you labour are not
produced by taxation. I have shown you that the whole expense of
the government, from the king to the common soldier, does not
amount to more than one halfpenny a day upon each individual in the
two kingdoms; and that the abolition of the whole of the government
would relieve you to the amount of only one halfpenny a day . . . and
I have told you that the immediate cause of your poverty is the
exorbitant rents, tithes, interests on money, profits on labour, and
profits of trade, which are imposed on you by laws made by the
landstealers, the merchants, the manufacturers and the tradesmen in   10
that house from which you are excluded and by which exclusion you
are prevented from making laws to regulate your wages.

Poor Man's Guardian, 14 April 1832

7.16   'Force and fraud'

The feudal and theological systems, the systems of force and fraud,

sometimes at war, sometimes at peace with each other, ruled the
affairs of men and consumed all the products of labour that were not
necessary to keep the labourers in existence and in working condition.
In the midst of these contentions of force and fraud, the system of   5
Industry working on knowledge has been gradually working its way.
In every part of Europe the system of Industry is partly established.
In no part of Europe, or in the world, is the system of Industry, as it
ought everywhere to be, predominant over the system of force and
fraud. Wars were formerly waged for rapine or superstition. During   10
the latter ages they have frequently been waged under the sincere
ignorant belief of procuring commercial advantages by them. So
much, however, are the old systems of force and fraud interwoven in
our present social arrangements, that there is scarcely a transaction of
life in which even at the present day, force and fraud do not take a   15
share . . . From the intricacies of production, the difficulties of
ascertaining value and quality, from the inequalities of knowledge and
skill, there is scarcely a transaction of barter or exchange in which the
over-reaching spirit of competition does not mingle fraud, whether by
an affected indifference to exchange, or by undervaluing the thing to   20
be acquired, or by overvaluing the thing to be given. By unjust
exchanges, then, supported by force or fraud, whether by direct
operation of law, or by indirect operation of unwise social
arrangements, are the products of the labour of the industrious classes
taken out of their hands. The field for chicane is unbounded as the   25
exercise of human faculties.

William Thompson, 'One of the Idle Classes', in *Labour Rewarded*,
1827

7.17   The Norman Yoke

Q. How has it originated that society has become divided into
labourers and idlers?
A. In the infancy of society every man exerted himself to supply his
own wants and for the common good; but in the process of time one
man assumed power over others and compelled others to keep him in   5
idleness; and thus was the natural state of society destroyed.
Q. Was this the case in Britain?
A. It was – A vile plunderer (called William the Conqueror) about
1000 years ago overran Britain and divided the soil amongst his

followers; and they in succession to the present time have found the labouring class to supply their wants.

The Pioneer, 5th October 1833

7.18 Need for institutional change

The object and right of the labourer is to get an equivalent for his labour, alias the full value of his produce in money. Whatever prevents him getting this value is, to him, robbery. The important question to him then is, what is it that prevents his getting that value? The answer is . . . the INSTITUTIONS OF THE COUNTRY. 5
These institutions give one portion of his earnings to the landlord, another to the parson, a third to the tax gatherer, a fourth to the lawyer, a fifth to the money lender, a sixth to the man of income . . . and a seventh (which is the largest share) to the capitalist – alias, to the parties who grow rich by setting him to work for them, or by 10
exchanging and selling his produce. How, whatever is given to, or rather taken by, these parties, beyond a fair equivalent for their respective services, is to him [the labourer] so much downright robbery.

Poor Man's Guardian, 14 February 1835

7.19 Exploitation

The factory system originated in robbery and was established in injustice . . . The factory masters have destroyed a race of the best and most intelligent class – the handloom weavers . . . English society has been so completely undermined and public confidence has been so destroyed by the accursed factory system that a despotic 5
government can introduce any measure, whether poor law or centralisation among them.

R. McDouall, a leading Chartist, in *The Northern Star*, 23 March 1839

7.20 Society as a beehive

'The state of the nation in Britain, 1840', cartoon by George
Cruickshank, 1840

Questions

1   What does the *Poor Man's Guardian* identify as the root cause of oppression [**7.15 and 7.18**]? In what ways is this viewpoint oversimplistic?

2   'Force and fraud'. How good a case does William Thompson make [**7.16**]?

3   What do you understand by the 'Norman Yoke' [**7.17**]? Why did contemporaries place such emphasis upon it?

4   Political oppression or economic exploitation? Which provides the better explanation for social conditions according to documents **7.15** to **7.19**?

5   Robbery, Rights, Repression. Why were these three Rs so important in the radical critique of early nineteenth–century society?

6   How convincing as a model of society do you find 'the beehive' [**7.20**]?

7   Is the model [**7.20**] paternalist or not?

The language used in the debate on the nature of society changed. 'Balance' gave way to 'exploitation', 'dependence' to 'robbery'. But was this a movement from paternalism to an idea of class? Deferential attitudes remained important throughout the nineteenth century and the idea of class has remained undigested in the British mind. Though the rural–urban divide was important in determining social attitudes, the distinction should not be pushed too far. There were factory owners who were as paternalist in attitude as their landowning contemporaries. Feelings of exploitation, oppression and fear existed among the rural labourers as well as the urban workers. The distinction between 'haves' and 'have-nots', rich and poor, spanned that divide. 'An abdication on the part of the governors' occurred in this period, Thomas Carlyle maintained. This placed severe strain upon the notion of mutual responsibility, the belief in the fairness and justice of the old hierarchical system. And yet Benjamin Disraeli is surely correct when he wrote in 1845 of,

> Two nations; between whom there is no intercourse and no sympathy; who are as ignorant of each other's habits, thought and feelings, as if they were dwellers in different zones, or inhabitants of different planets; who are formed by a different breeding, are fed by a different food, are ordered by different manners and are not governed by the same laws.

It was not that society had ceased to be caring, it had ceased to know itself.

Index